Facts, Stats & Trivia of
The Melbourne Cup

VICTORIA RACING CLUB
SPRING MEETING
1959

MELBOURNE CUP
TUESDAY, 3rd NOVEMBER

OFFICIAL
PROGRAMME

Price **2/-**

Facts, Stats & Trivia of
The Melbourne Cup

Paddy O'Reilly

NEW
HOLLAND

SPORTS NOVELS
For NOVEMBER
2/-

Registered at the General Post Office, Sydney, for transmission by post as a periodical.

"Dalray"

"Delta"

8 EXTRA PAGES

Melbourne Cup Special !

"Hydrogen"

"Grey Boots"

Introduction

The Melbourne Cup has long been the 'race that stops the nation', but increasingly it has become the race the entire world stops to watch. From humble beginnings in the 1860s when a two mile horserace, conducted under handicap conditions, brought the fledgling colony of Melbourne together, the Melbourne Cup has developed into a quality international race that attracts the best stayers from around the world.

What is it then about a horserace that can hold such a special place? What does this say about us as nation of people, that we willingly down tools on the first Tuesday in November and have a bet on a horse race? Hopefully, it says a lot about our egalitarian nature rather than our love of 'a punt' but it's clear horseracing is in our DNA. Better writers than me have reflected that life is very much like the Melbourne Cup – there are handicaps to carry and barriers to overcome, and the best horse doesn't always win – but it is a two mile race, and you don't win the Melbourne Cup the first time you run down the straight. There is another lap ... so keep going, keep trying! Don't make your run too early and save something for the finish!

And that's the idea behind this little book. Having assembled all the facts and trivia, and separated the myths from the documented history, I trust the reader will appreciate the many stories and records that have built up over time. All the great names are here ... Carbine, Phar Lap, Peter Pan, Rising Fast, Rain Lover, Think Big, Let's Elope and Makybe Diva. There's a few names you may not have heard of too ... do you remember Tim Whiffler, know the story of Nimblefoot or appreciate what a good horse The Trump was? No? Then read on and enjoy!

I might even be able to point you in the direction of backing a winner or two in the years ahead, but I trust this book becomes a handy reference guide and a ready argument settler for the guys in the pub!

Patrick 'Paddy' O'Reilly

Record Spot

Slowest Winning Time

3:52.00 - Archer (1861)

Lantern (1864)

Biggest Winning Margin

8 lengths - Archer (1862)

Rain Lover (1968)

Did You Know?

The runners in the inaugural Melbourne Cup in 1861 did not compete for a Cup or trophy. The only prize was the £910 winner's purse – with a lowly £20 allocated for second place – on offer. The first Cup trophy was not awarded until 1865 and the eponymous three-handled gold cup was not struck until 1938.

History Spot

Archer
(1861)

Archer won the inaugural Melbourne Cup, a two-mile handicap race conducted by the then Victory Turf Club, on Thursday, November 7, 1861. The winning time of 3 minutes 52 seconds remains the slowest on record. Three horses fell (two were destroyed) and a fourth (Twilight) bolted before the race and did a lap of the racetrack, but was allowed to start.

Contrary to popular myth, Archer was not walked the 500 miles (800 km) from his Nowra training track on NSW's south coast to Melbourne's Flemington racecourse. Trainer Etienne de Mestre sent Archer by ship, as per the usual transportation mode of the time, but it's a good story.

Ridden by Johnny 'Cutts' Dillon, Archer provided de Mestre with the first of a then record five Cup winners when he romped home by 6 lengths. Archer started at the odds of 6–1 in defeating local hope Mormon (W. Simpson) with Prince two lengths away in third place.

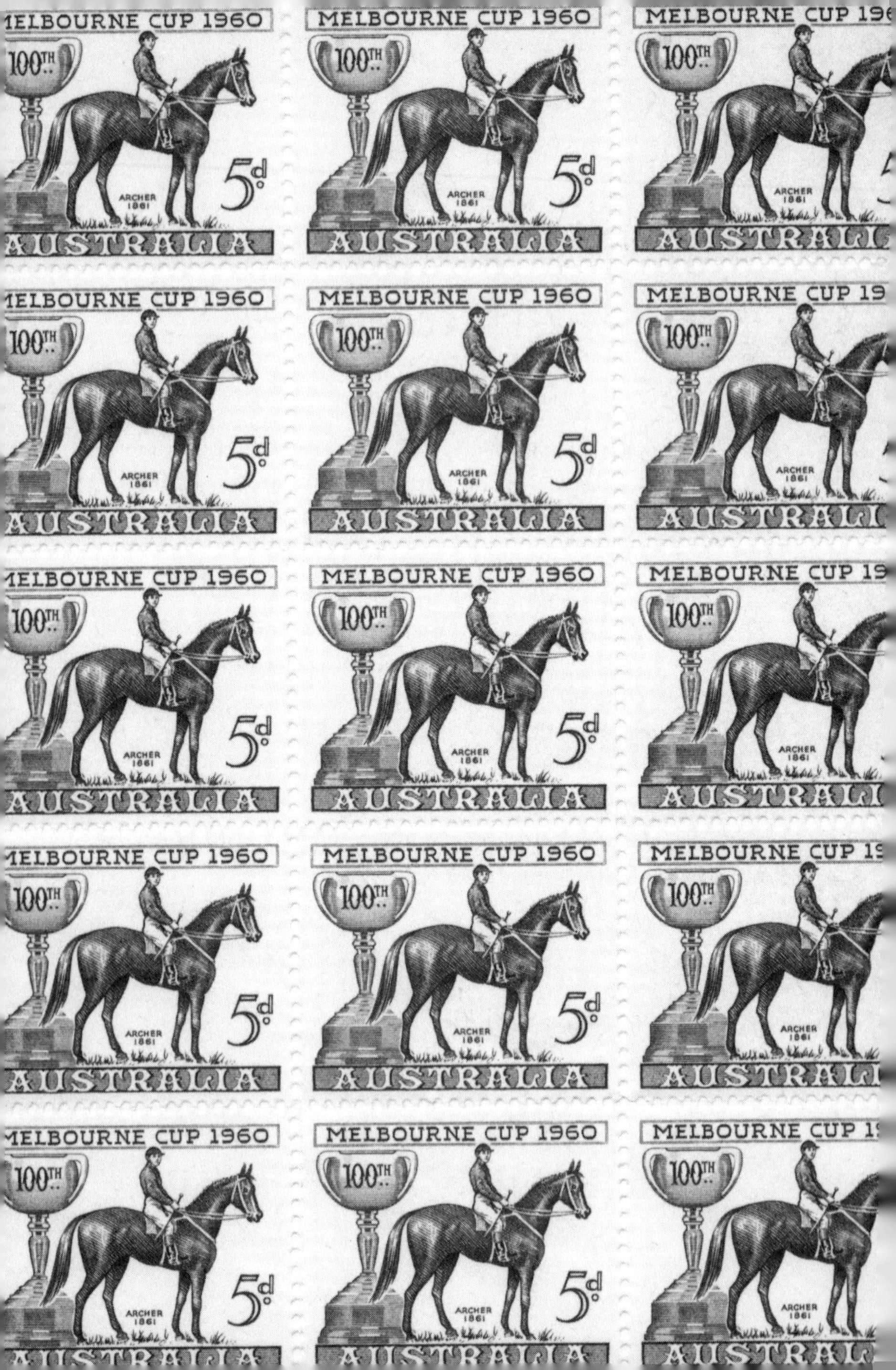
MELBOURNE CUP 1960
100TH
ARCHER
1861
5d
AUSTRALIA

History Spot

Archer
(1862)

Twelve months after its victory in the inaugural running of the race, Archer returned to Melbourne in 1862 and captured his second Melbourne Cup, defeating Mormon for a second successive time by the record margin of eight lengths.

Archer carried 10st 12lb (64.5kg), a record weight that would stand until Carbine's victory in 1890. Archer was again ridden by Johnny Cutts, whose real name was John 'Cutts' Dillon (1829–1872). Myth makers would have us believe that Cutts was of Aboriginal descent, but this is not the case. Frank Reys (Gala Supreme, 1973) was the first jockey of Aboriginal descent to win the Cup.

Archer may have won the first three Cups, but an administrative error on 1 July, 1863 resulted in its entry arriving in Melbourne a day late and the Victoria Turf Club vetoed his inclusion. Archer was to carry the impost of 11st 4lb (almost 72kg), which would have been a record if successful.

Opposite: 1861–62 Melbourne Cup winner Archer featured on the centenary stamp which was released in 1960.

Record Spot

Lightest Weight

5 stone 4lb (33.5kg)	Banker (1863)

Smallest Field

7	Banker (1863)

Did You Know?

The Melbourne Cup started under the auspices of the Victoria Turf Club in 1861. Originally inaugurated to promote the fledgling colony of Melbourne, the early years of the race's history was plagued by rivalry between Melbourne's two race clubs – the Victorian Turf Club and the Victoria Jockey Club. Mismanagement and lack of promotion resulted in just seven runners taking their place in the 1863 Cup for record low prize money. The following year, the Victoria Racing Club came into being after the two rival clubs were disbanded and the VRC took over the administrations of the Cup.

History Spot

Banker
(1863)

Banker, ridden by H. Chifney, set a number of records when he won the 1863 Melbourne Cup. The race attracted only seven runners, the smallest field in the history of the race, and Banker set a record for carrying the lightest weight – 5st (33.5kg).

Trained by Sam Waldcot, Banker also became the first three-year-old colt to win the two-mile handicap, although he was not the VRC Derby winner that year. Banker defeated his better performing older brother Barwon (Barlodo-Jeanette) in the Cup, which carried top weight in the race.

Banker, which was the outsider of the small field starting at 10/1, defeated joint favourites Musidora and Rose of Denmark (both 2/1). The 1863 Cup reflected the dire straits Melbourne racing was in at the time, with the Cup's lowest first prize on offer of just £510.

Record Spot

Victoria Derby – Melbourne Cup as a three-year-old

1864	Lantern *
1876	Briseis
1877	Chester
1880	Grand Flaneur
1883	Martini-Henri
1896	Newhaven
1899	Meriwee
1906	Poseidon
1909	Prince Foote
1915	Patrobas
1927	Trivalve
1933	Hall Mark
1941	Skipton

Did You Know?

Lantern won the Melbourne Cup first, followed by the Derby, as the races were then programmed. Originally, the Melbourne Cup Carnival started on Saturday and then continued on Thursday (Cup Day), Friday (Derby Day) and concluded on Saturday (Oaks Day).

In 1875, the VRC rejigged the Melbourne Cup carnival with Derby Day run on the first Saturday, followed by the Cup on Tuesday, the Oaks on Thursday and concluding the following Saturday. It's been that way ever since.

History Spot

Lantern
(1864)

L antern started a proud tradition of VRC Derby winners which were Melbourne Cup winners in the same year, except that the colt achieved the feat the wrong way around! In 1864, under the newly formed Victoria Race Club (VRC), The Melbourne Cup was held on a Thursday, the day before the VRC Derby.

Starting at 15/1, Lantern powered through a heavy shower of rain with its light weight (6st 3lb/39.5kg) to defeat favourite Poet by one and a half lengths, with the 1863 placegetter, Rose of Demark, again running third. The heavy going saw Lantern equal Archer's slowest ever race time of 3 minutes and 52 seconds.

Lantern's trainer S. Mahon backed the colt up the following day and won the VRC Derby by six lengths. On the Saturday, Lantern won the mile (1600m) Bookmaker's Purse, proving both his versatility and endurance. Tragically, Lantern broke down and had to be destroyed only days later, competing in the Ballarat Cup.

Record Spot

Multiple Cups Contested

6	Shadow King
	1929 (6th)
	1930 (3rd)
	1931 (2nd)
	1932 (3rd)
	1933 (2nd)
	1935 (4th)
5	Toryboy, Strop, Barwon, Musidora, Skybeau, Red Cadeaux

Did You Know?

Toryboy, Musidora and Barwon competed against each other on multiple occasions during the Cup's first decade. All three horses started in five Melbourne Cups – a record only bettered by perennial placegetter Shadow King (1929–1935).

Toryboy won the Melbourne Cup in 1865 on his third try (also 1861–62 and 1866–67). Musidora ran second to Banker in the 1863 Cup after finishing unplaced in 1862. She also contested the 1866–67 Cups and, retired to stud, was the dam of 1876 Cup winner Briseis. Barwon ran in five Cups (1861, 1863, 1864, 1866 and 1867) but was unplaced on each occasion.

History Spot

Toryboy
(1865)

For the first time in its history, the VRC awarded a trophy to the connections of the Melbourne Cup winner in 1865. Manufactured in England, it was an elaborate silver bowl on a stand with a narrow neck reinforced with two ornate handles and topped with a horse and rider. The winning owner, Mr B.C. Marshall, later sold the trophy, which he considered 'a monstrosity'.

Toryboy, an eight-year-old grey gelding, won the 1865 Melbourne at 25/1 for jockey Eugene Cavanagh and trainer Mr P. Miley. It was the first time a grey horse and an eight-year-old won the Cup. Panic, the runner-up in the race, actually protested against the winner but this was quickly dismissed. The protest was hopeful at best, with Toryboy making the most of his 3st (19kg) weight advantage, surging to a four-length win.

Record Spot

AJC Derby – Melbourne Cup at 3 years

1866	The Barb
1880	Grand Flaneur
1906	Poseidon
1909	Prince Foote
1932	Peter Pan
1933	Hall Mark

Did You Know?

Only six winners of the AJC Derby have won the Melbourne Cup in the same calendar year as a three-year-old. This was at a time when the AJC Derby was held in the Spring, and colts would continue on to Melbourne for the Derby and the Cup after the Sydney Spring Carnival.

In 1979, the AJC Derby was moved to the Autumn so it is no longer possible for a three-year-old to win both races in the same calendar year. It is even rarer for three-year-olds to contest the Melbourne Cup, so the likelihood of a Melbourne Cup winner capturing the AJC Derby the following year is extremely rare.

Interestingly, Phar Lap remains the only AJC Derby winner (1929) to go on to win the Melbourne Cup as an older horse (1930). Tulloch (1957 AJC Derby) tried and failed (1960), Kingston Town (1980 AJC Derby) ran second in 1982 and Criterion (2014 AJC Derby) ran third in the 2015 Cup.

History Spot

The Barb
(1866)

Such was The Barb's domination of racing in the late 1860s the Sydney colt was called 'The Black Demon'. As well as becoming the first AJC Derby winner to win the Melbourne Cup, The Barb also won the race at only his sixth start in a race. The Barb started 6/1 favourite and won by a head from Exile, with Falcon declared third the following day after the VRC judge declined to make a decision! *

The Barb went on to win the Metropolitan Hcp (1868), two Sydney Cups (1868 and 1869, the second carrying 10st 8lb!) and was all but unbeatable at weight-for-age. In the Melbourne Cup of 1869, The Barb was allotted top-weight with a record 11st 8lb (73.5kg) – the highest weight given to any horse in the race's history – but did not start and was retired to stud.

* Two horses named Falcon competed in the 1866 Melbourne Cup and the judge did not recognise the placegetter's colours, which were different to the official program.

Record Spot

Successful Trainers

5 wins	Etienne De Mestre
	Archer (1861-62)
	Tim Whiffler (1867)
	Chester (1877)
	Calamia (1878)

Did you know?

Etienne de Mestre (1832–1916) held the record for almost 100 years as the Melbourne Cup's most successful trainer with five wins. De Mestre set up his training and stud complex on the Shoalhaven River on NSW's south coast in the 1850s and had almost immediate success. He won three of the first seven Melbourne Cup contested, and added to his record with the success of Chester (1870) and Calamia (1978). De Mestre may have added to his record had Cup favourite Robin Hood not drowned at sea on his way to Melbourne in 1876.

An inveterate gambler, de Mestre encountered financial and health problems in later years and his properties and stock were auctioned off to pay his debts in 1883. When other investments soured, friends and racing acquaintances organised a benefit for him and he was able to live out a long life quietly in Moss Vale, NSW.

Tim Whiffler
(1867)

In 1867, two horses named Tim Whiffler competed in the Melbourne Cup. To distinguish between the two horses, bookmakers referred to the horses as 'Melbourne Tim' and 'Sydney Tim'. 'Sydney Tim', the AJC Derby winner, was trained by Etienne de Mestre and won by two lengths as the 5/2 favourite. 'Melbourne Tim' finished fifth. Exile, the previous year's runner-up, ran third.

A silver trophy displaying Alexander the Great 'taming the horse' and a figure of a winged female, by Thomas Smily of London firm W.R. Smily & Company, was awarded to Tim Whiffler's owner. Tim Whiffler's Melbourne Cup trophy, and the Queen's Plate trophy the horse won leading up to its success in the 1867 Cup, are held in the National Museum of Australia.

'Sydney Tim' was retired to stud where his son – also called Tim Whiffler – won the Great Northern Derby in New Zealand in 1881.

Did You Know?

Tim Whiffler was the name of a ship that brought emigrants from London to Brisbane in the 1860s and 1870s. An English sire, also named Tim Whiffler, was later brought to Australia and sired the Melbourne Cup winners Briseis (1876) and Darriwell (1879).

Record Spot

Seven Letters in Winning Name

1864	Lantern	1865	Toryboy
1866	The Barb	1868	Glencoe
1869	Warrior	1873	Don Juan
1874	Haricot	1877	Chester
1878	Calamia	1886	Arsenal
1890	Carbine	1895	Auraria
1901	Revenue	1904	Acrasia
1912	Piastre	1916	Sasanof
1920	Poitrel	1923	Bitalli
1925	Windbag	1930	Phar Lap
1935	Marabou	1939	Rivette
1941	Skipton	1942	Colonus
1948	Rimfire	1953	Wodalla
1958	Toparoa	1966	Galilee
1979	Hyperno	1986	At Talaq
1992	Subzero	1996	Saintly
2011	Dunaden		

Did You Know?

What's in a name?

'Lucky 7' has long been a favoured number for gamblers, and it's no different with owners and backers of racehorses. Having seven letters in a horse's name was considered good luck in the 1800s and no less than 12 of the first 40 Melbourne Cup winners – just under a third – had seven letters in their name. The superstition faded in the late 20th Century (22 winners, or just over one fifth of all winners have seven letters in their name), although the 1920s trainer of a NZ gelding famously changed the number of letters in its name – from 'far lap', the Thai word for lightning, to Phar Lap – to ensure good luck. It worked!

Dunaden (2011) is the only horse with seven letters in its name to salute judge in the new millennium. Ed. note: the maximum number of characters allowed in a horse name is 18 (including spaces). Prince of Penzance (2015) used all 18 characters – the first Cup winner to do so.

History Spot

Nimblefoot
(1870)

Nimblefoot's win in 1870 has become an important part of Melbourne Cup folklore. According to the story, Ballarat publican Walter Craig bought the well-performed horse from Melbourne bookmaker Joe Thompson and sent him back to Tasmania to race under guidance of trainer W. Lang in an effort to recapture its best form. The seven-year-old gelding was originally given 6st (38kg) in the Melbourne Cup, but carried 6st 3lb (39.5kg) upon receiving a penalty after winning the Hotham Handicap.

Some months before the 1870 Melbourne Cup, Craig dreamt that a horse carrying his colours won the race, but with the jockey wearing a black arm band. Craig told some of his pub patrons about the dream and was sure that Nimblefoot would win the Cup, but he would not live to see it. When Craig suddenly died, the story was reported in the Melbourne Age on the day before the Cup. Jockey J. Day duly wore a band of black crepe on his arm as a mark of respect and rode Nimblefoot to victory at the odds of 12/1 after a tense battle with runner-up Lapdog.

Did You Know?

The entire 1870 Melbourne Cup carnival was postponed a week because the Flemington track was waterlogged. The Cup was also postponed in 1916 because of rain.

During the Second World War, the Cup was held on Saturday in 1942–44 because Flemington racetrack was being used a military camp.

Record Spot

Did You Know?

The Pearl (1871) was the first 100/1 winner of the Melbourne Cup. Punters backed his stablemate Pyrrhus in that race, completely overlooking The Pearl's good second in the AJC Metropolitan earlier in the Spring. Since then, only three other horses have won the race at this outsider price, the latest being Prince of Penzance in 2015.

Wotan (1936) was certainly poorly performed – finishing second last in the WS Cox Plate – but the NZ-bred horse ran a new race record (3.21.25) in winning the Cup. Old Rowley was unplaced in the Hotham Handicap in his final hit-out before the Cup and had not won a race during his current preparation, but no doubt his stout breeding (by The Buzzard, the same sire as 1945 winner Rainbird) kept him in good stead in the run to the post.

In 2015, Prince of Penzance ran a great second to The United States in the Mooney Valley Cup in its final lead up race but was unwanted in betting largely because the gelding had a female jockey on board.

Record Spot

Most wins by an owner

4	John Tait (1866, 1868, 1871, 1872)
	Etienne de Mestre (1861*, 1862*, 1867*, 1878)
	Dato Tan Chin Nam (1974, 1975, 1996, 2008)
	Lloyd Williams (1981, 1985, 2007, 2012)

* The winners of these Cups were leased. De Mestre did not own Chester, which he trained to win the 1877 Melbourne Cup.

Did You Know?

John Tait (1813–1888) jointly holds the record for most Cup winners by an owner, and also trained his four winners – The Barb (1866), Glencoe (1868), The Pearl (1871) and The Quack (1872). Born in Scotland, Tait saw racing as a business and closely supervised his training (Randwick) and stud (Mount Druitt) establishments. Known as "Honest John" Tait, when his champion The Barb defeated the Etienne de Mestre's Tim Whiffler in 1868 Queen's Plate, only to be disqualified for weighing in light, Tait offered a £100 reward for any evidence of 'skulduggery'.

In becoming the owner of four Cup winners, Tait's record was equalled by his rival Etienne de Mestre in 1878, and in modern times, by millionaire owners Dato Tan Chin Nam and Lloyd Williams. While Tan Chin Nam was happy to let Bart Cummings do his training for him, Lloyd Williams has taken very much a hands-on role in the preparation of his last two Cup winners after being a part owner in Just a Dash (1981) and What a Nuisance (1985).

Don Juan
(1873)

Don Juan's victory in the 1873 was shrouded in controversy. Trained by James Wilson at his newly established St Alban's Stud near Geelong, Don Juan started the 3/1 favourite in the race and won with ease, by three lengths in race record time, to reap a punting bonanza for its connections. That's when the trouble started.

Don Juan was entered under the ownership of Mr W. Johnstone, who was paid £100 to act as a front for bookmaker Joe Thompson. When the four-year-old horse struck form in the lead up to the Cup, Thompson and Wilson backed Don Juan for a fortune. The Thompson-Wilson camp had overlooked the fact that Don Juan was on a private sale list, however, and the four-year-old was bought by Mr J. Inglis for 500 guineas. Realising his error, Thompson persuaded Inglis to allow him to continue to lease the horse until after the Cup. After Don Juan's victory, Thompson bought the horse back from Inglis for 2,000 guineas.

Immediately following Don Juan's victory, a protest was fired in from rival bookmakers that the horse was actually a year older than stated (Don Juan had carried a featherweight 6st 12lb or 43.5kg in the win). Worse still, rumours spread throughout the racing industry that Don Juan had been substituted for a better-performing horse from the leading stable. The protest was later dismissed, the rumour never proven, and stewards satisfied that Don Juan was what they said it was ... a Cup winner!

Record Spot

Fillies to win the Melbourne Cup

1876	Briseis
1895	Auraria
1921	Sister Olive

Did You Know?

Only three three-year-old fillies have won the Melbourne Cup. In today's era, it would be unthinkable that a three-year-old filly, untried over two miles, would tackle the Cup before the VRC Oaks (2500 m) which is traditionally run two days after the Melbourne Cup. Very few fillies even run in the VRC Derby, with Frances Tressady (1923), the last of the fairer sex to defeat the boys in the Derby.

Auraria had finished third in the VRC Derby on the Saturday before her Cup victory in 1895, but still started at the good odds of 33/1. Two days later, she showed her class by winning the VRC Oaks and then backed up to dead-heat with Wallace, a champion son of Carbine, in the CB Fisher Plate on the last day of the Melbourne Cup carnival.

Sister Olive (1921) is the last of the three-year-old fillies to win the Cup. The filly won only one race before her Cup success, as a two-year-old in the Maribyrnong Plate, but a good fourth in the Caulfield Cup saw her sent out a 16/1 chance in the Cup. Sister Olive then ran third in the VRC Oaks (to the champion Furious, which also won the VRC Derby) and competed in two more Cups (1922-23) but never won another race.

History Spot

Briseis
(1876)

The youngest jockey to win the Melbourne Cup was Peter St. Albans on Briseis in 1876. St. Albans, whose real name was Michael Bowden (1863–1898), was just shy of his thirteenth birthday when he won the Cup. Bowden took his surname from the training complex where he worked to mask the fact that he was not officially old enough to ride in the Cup.

Brisies became the first three-year-old filly to capture the Melbourne Cup, but also the only horse to win the VRC Derby-Cup-VRC Oaks treble during Melbourne Cup week. Briseis started at 13/2 in the Cup and defeated Sibyl by two lengths with Timothy a length away in third place. Briseis was an exceptionally gifted filly, having won the AJC Doncaster as a two-year-old!

Briseis never won another race after the 1876 Cup success, however, and was retired to stud duties. Unfortunately, the mare struck her head while being served by the stallion King of the Ring in 1879 and tragically died without producing any progeny.

Did You Know?

The first Cup trophy manufactured in Victoria was awarded to the connections of Briseis in 1876. An Etruscan shaped trophy with two handles, made in Australia by Austrian immigrant Edward Fischer, one side depicts a picture of a horse race with the grandstand and hill of Flemington in the background. The opposite side, inscribed on a crimson enamelled garter, features the words 'Melbourne Cup 1876' and the name Briseis.

"GRAND FLANEUR" YATTENDON — FIRST LADY.

History Spot

Grand Flaneur
(1880)

Grand Flaneur holds the distinction of being the only undefeated winner of the Melbourne Cup. After capturing the AJC Derby at only his second start, Grand Flaneur won the VRC Derby at his fourth start, defeating the James Wilson-trained Progress. Grand Flaneur would beat Progress on all five occasions they met, including their next clash in the 1880 Melbourne Cup.

Progress, ridden by Peter St Albans, started 3/1 favourite in the Cup, but Grand Flaneur (4/1) conceded him a stone in weight and beat him by a length. Ridden by the great Tommy Hales, Grand Flaneur followed up its Cup win with victory in the Mares Produce Stakes. Progress ran third.

After winning three more races in the Autumn of 1881, Grand Flaneur (Yattendon – First Lady) was retired to stud after breaking down with the unbeaten record of 9 wins and £8,105 in stakes. Grand Flaneur was leading Australian sire in the 1894–95 seasons and his sons, Patron (1894) and Bravo (1889) won Melbourne Cups.

Opposite: A rare photo of the great Grand Flaneur at stud in the 1880s; and (above) as drawn in local newspapers during his racing career.

Record Spot

Winning by Alphabet (First letter)

A	10	(Americain 2010)
B	11	(Black Knight 1984)
C	8	(Comic Court 1950)
D	9	(Dunaden 2011)
E	5	(Efficient 2007)
F	2	(Fiorente 2013)
G	10	(Green Moon 2012)
H	5	(Hyperno 1979)
I	0	(no winner)
J	5	(Jezabeel 1998)
K	6	(Kingston Rule 1990)
L	6	(Let's Elope 1991)
M	12	(Makybe Diva 2005)
N	4	(Nightmarch 1929)
O	1	(Old Rowley 1940)
P	14	(Prince of Penzance 2015)
Q	0	(no winner)
R	10	(Rogan Josh 1999)
S	12	(Shocking 2009)
T	15	(Tawriffic 1989)
U	0	(No Winner)
V	3	(Viewed 2008)
W	8	(What a Nuisance 1985)
X	0	(no Winner)
Y	0	(no Winner)
Z	1	(Zulu 1881)

Did You Know?

Zulu (1881) is the only winner of the Cup whose names starts with 'Z' (Ziema ran second in 1965 and Zazabelle equal third in 1999). During the 1881 Cup, a dog ran onto the course causing three horses to fall and the death of jockey John Dodd (on the former 1879 placegetter Suwarrow).

The most popular letter of the alphabet for Melbourne Cup winners is 'T', although this can be partially explained by the number of Cup winners with the prefix 'The' in their name which was popular in the first half of the race's history – The Trump (1937), The Parisian (1911), The Victory (1902), The Grafter (1898), The Assyrian (1882), The Quack (1872), The Pearl (1871) and The Barb (1866).

No Melbourne Cup winner has had a name that started with the letters 'X' (not so surprisingly), 'Y' (Yippyio ran second in 2000), 'U', 'O' or 'I'. So if you're thinking of naming your Melbourne Cup hopeful 'Up the ..', 'On the ... ' or 'In the...' think again. You'll be taking on history if you do.

Record Spot

New Zealand-bred winners

1883	Martini-Henry	1970	Baghdad Note*
1890	Carbine	1971	Silver Knight*
1907	Apologue	1974-75	Think Big
1916	Sasanof*	1976	Van der Hum*
1929	Nightmarch*	1977	Gold and Black
1930	Phar Lap	1978	Arwon
1936	Wotan*	1979	Hyperno
1938	Catalogue*	1982	Gurner's Lane
1947	Hiraji	1983	Kiwi*
1949	Foxzami	1985	What a Nuisance
1952	Dalray*	1987	Kensei
1954	Rising Fast*	1988	Empire Rose*
1955	Toparoa	1989	Tawrrific
1957	Straight Draw	1991	Let's Elope
1959	Macdougal	1995	Doriemus
1960	Hi Jinx*	1997	Might and Power
1962	Even Stevens*	1998	Jezabeel*
1964	Polo Prince*	2000	Brew*
1965	Light Fingers	2001	Ethereal*
1966	Galilee	2007	Efficient
1967	Red Handed	2015	Prince of Penzance

* New Zealand-trained

Just over a quarter of all Melbourne Cup winners (27.1%) have been bred in New Zealand. From Martini-Henri in 1883 to Prince of Penzance in 2015, racehorses from the 'Shaky Isles' have continued to rewrite the record books. It is believed that a combination of New Zealand's quiet rural studs, lime-enriched soil and large open paddocks contributed to the development of great 'stayers', while Australia's move towards sprint breeds in the 1970s left the breeding of staying stock behind.

Most gallingly for 'Aussie' sports fans Phar Lap, arguably our greatest horse, was bred in New Zealand, along with other notable champions Carbine (1890), Rising Fast (1954), Let's Elope (1991) and Ethereal (2001). Champion trainer Bart Cummings was a particular fan of New Zealand-bred horses, with his first six Cup winners coming from across the Tasman (Light Fingers 1965, Galilee 1966, Red Handed 1967, Think Big 1974–75, Arwon 1978 and Hyperno 1979).

Alas, the arrival of foreign-bred horses competing in the Melbourne Cup has taken the gloss off the New Zealand breeding scene as far as the Melbourne Cup is concerned, but our 'little brothers' across the Tasman continue to bat above their weight when it comes to producing Melbourne Cup winners.

Did You Know?

New Zealand-bred horses filled all three placings in six Melbourne Cups – 1929 (Nightmarch/Paquito/Phar Lap), 1955 (Toparoa/Rising Fast/Sir William), 1960 (Hi Jinx/Howsie/Ilumquh), 1974 (Think Big/ Leilani/Captain Peri), 1975 (Think Big/ Holiday Wagon/Medici) and 1978 (Arwon/Dandaleith/Karu)

Martini-Henri
(1883)

New Zealand bred Martini-Henri won the VRC Derby and its first race start and backed up three days later to capture the Melbourne Cup in only his second race. The son of Musket (later the sire of Carbine) then rounded off the Melbourne Cup Carnival with a win the Mares Produce Stakes on the Monday (postponed from Saturday). Martin-Henri was also a short-priced favourite for the AJC Derby earlier in the Spring, but an injury setback saw his trainer Michael Fennelley target the Melbourne Carnival.

Martin-Henri started 5/1 favourite in the Melbourne Cup and beat First Water by one and a half lengths with Commotion third. The colt won the VRC St. Leger in the Autumn before breaking down in the Caulfield Cup later that year and being retired to stud.

Did You Know?

Martini-Henri was not only the first New Zealand-bred horse to win the Cup, but it remains the only Cup winner to have a hyphen in its name. The hyphen is important too ... the Martini–Henry was a breech-loading single-shot lever-actuated rifle used by the British Army. It first entered service in 1871, and became famous for its use in the Anglo-Zulu wars in South Africa in 1879. Interestingly, Zulu won the 1881 Melbourne Cup just two years before Martini-Henri.

History Spot

Malua
(1884)

Malua must certainly go down as the most versatile Melbourne Cup winner in history. Originally named Bagot in its native Tasmania where it was bred in 1879, the horse was sold in Melbourne at the end of its two-year-old season and renamed Malua, which is a Fijian word that means 'to linger'. Malua won the Newmarket Handicap-Oakleigh Plate sprint double in the Autumn of 1884, before capturing the Adelaide Cup over two miles!

Malua won the Melbourne Stakes (later Mackinnon Stakes) in his final lead up to the 1884 Melbourne Cup. Carrying 9st 9lb (61kg) Malua started at 6/1 and hauled in top-weight Commotion, which had run third in the previous years' Cup, to win by a half-length. Two days later, Malua was beaten a head by the two-year-old Newstead in the six furlongs (1200m) Flying Stakes.

Malua finished off his racing career by winning the Grand National Hurdle in 1887. At stud, he sired the 1891 Melbourne Cup winner Malvolio.

Record Spot

Successful Trainers

4 wins	Walter Hickenbotham
	Mentor (1888)
	Carbine (1890)
	Newhaven (1896)
	Blue Spec (1905)

Did You Know?

Pat Reynold, the lessee of the Royal Mail Hotel in Bourke Street, Melbourne, presented jockey Mick O'Brien with a gold-mounted whip to mark his winning Cup ride on the Walter Hickenbotham-trained Mentor in 1888. The following year, this was continued by the Wirth brothers whose circus was located on the land now occupied by the Victorian Arts Centre. The whip presentation was made to the winning jockey in the circus centre ring on Cup night. When Wirth's Circus closed, the family continued presenting Wirth's Whip on Cup night for many years.

History Spot

Mentor
(1888)

The Walter Hickenbotham-trained Mentor won the Centennial Melbourne Cup of 1888, so named because it was conducted in the year of celebration for the centenary of Australia's founding. The VRC boosted prize money to £3,000 and the Cup trophy comprised a set of three silver horse figurines on a silver-plated base.

Mentor ran out a comfortable 7/1 winner for popular jockey Mick O'Brien and was the first of four Cup wins for Walter Hickenbotham (1848–1930). Among the beaten brigade was Bravo, from Ballarat, which returned twelve months later to win the 1889 Cup.

Mentor's owner Donald Wallace collected £20,000 in winning bets on his horse and bought a New Zealand-bred colt for 3,000 guineas which was a certainty beaten in the VRC Derby in 1889. The horse's name was Carbine.

Record Spot

Heaviest Weight

10st 5lb (66kg)	Carbine (1890)

Largest Field

39	Carbine (1890)

Did You Know?

More than a 125 years after Carbine carried a record 10st 5lb/65.5kg to victory in the 1890 Melbourne Cup, the weight is unlikely to be bettered. Phar Lap (9st 12lb /62.5kg in 1930) is the closest weighted winner to Carbine. Phar Lap carried 10st 10lb/68kg in the 1931 Melbourne Cup but did not run a place.

A trophy of a silver ewer, salver and tazzas was awarded to the owners of Carbine, after the 1890 Melbourne Cup. The set was bought at auction by the VRC in 2000 for $272,500 and is on display at the National Sports Museum at the MCG in Melbourne.

History Spot

Carbine
(1890)

Carbine stands only in the shadow of the immortal Phar Lap as the greatest racehorse ever produced in Australasia. Foaled in New Zealand in 1885, the son of Musket (GB) won 33 of his 43 race starts including the 1890 Melbourne Cup and two Sydney Cups (1889 and 1890). After running second to Bravo in the 1889 Cup, Carbine carried a record weight to victory over a capacity field in record time. Ridden by Bob Ramage, Carbine won by two and a half lengths from Highborn, which carried the luxury weight of 6st 6lb (41kg).

Retired to stud, 'Old Jack' as the horse was known around the stables, proved a sensation. More than half of the 65 Melbourne Cup winners from 1911–1878 have Carbine in their pedigree. Carbine was later purchased by the Duke of Portland for 13,000 guineas and stood at stud in England.

History Spot

Glenloth
(1892)

Melbourne milkman James Urquhart bought a horse with the help of a winning Caulfield–Melbourne Cup double in 1890 (Vengeance–Carbine). The colt Glenloth, named after a little town in north-western Victoria, was in good form and was secured for £400. A noted mudlark, Glenloth relished the conditions in the 1892 Melbourne Cup after a heavy downpour delayed the start by 20 minutes.

The five-year-old started at 50/1 and won by three lengths on a quagmire track. Malvolio, the previous year's winner, was the unplaced 6/1 favourite. After the race, an intricate 17in (45cm) trophy was presented to Urquhart. In 2007, the great-great-granddaughter of the horse's breeder paid $140,000 for the 1892 Cup trophy at auction.

Did You Know?

Famed American writer Mark Twain visited Melbourne in 1895 as part of his world speaking tour to stave off financial ruin after his failed business ventures and attended the Cup won by the filly Auraria. 'The Melbourne Cup is the Australasian National Day,' he later wrote. 'It would be difficult to overstate its importance. It overshadows all other holidays and specialised days of whatever sort in that congeries of colonies. Overshadows them? I might almost say it blots them out.'

Did You Know?

The Melbourne Cup in 1896 was the first to be filmed. Marius Sestier and Henry Walter Barnett filmed scenes during the Melbourne Cup Carnival that year, producing one of Australia's oldest surviving films. Barnett, the producer of this film, encouraged the crowd to wave their hats as the horses came down the straight to the finish line with Newhaven in the lead. The film was later shown around the country.

GAULUS

Did You Know?

Gaulus (1897) and The Grafter (1898) were full brothers, being by Gozo out of the Musket mare Industry (NZ). Both were owned and trained by Mr W. Forrester, with the older brother Gaulus defeating The Grafter in the 1897 Cup by half a head. The following year, The Grafter beat Wait-a-Bit by a half neck.

Trophies were not awarded to the owners of Patron, Auraria, Newhaven, Gaulus and The Grafter in the late 1890s because of the economic depression. Prizemoney for the Cup fell from £13,000 to just £5,000.

The Victory, 1902.

THE ADMIRAL — THE CHARMER.

B G. 4 years.   Weight, 8.12.   Time, 3.29.

Owners: Trainer: Jockey:

Clark & Robinson.   R. Bradfield.   R. W. Lewis.

2nd Vanity Fair 7.9; 3rd Abundance 7.6.

Starters, 22.   Starting price, 25 to 1.

Colors—Lavender, rose sleeves, collar and cap.

Record Spot

Most Successful Jockeys

4	Bobby Lewis*
	The Victory (1902)
	Patrobas (1915)
	Artilleryman (1919)
	Trivalve (1927)

* tied with Harry White

Did You Know?

Jockey Bobby Lewis (1878–1947) jointly holds the record for most Cup wins with four, spread over a 25 year period. His first win was on The Victory in 1902. Lewis had a 40 year association with trainer James Scobie, but only rode one of the trainer's four Melbourne Cup winners (Clean Sweep 1902, King Ingoda 1922, Bitalli 1923, and Trivalve 1927).

At age 49, Lewis wasted his already taut frame to make the weight of 7st 6lb (47kg) to ride Trivalve to victory. Lewis could easily have bettered his record of four wins from 33 Cup mounts (also five minor placings). In 1900, he was offered the ride on eventual winner Clean Sweep by Scobie but chose to stick with dual Derby winner Malster, which ran second. In 1929, Lewis rode the even-money favourite Phar Lap into a controversial third place after fighting the horse for much of the two miles but was unable to get the budding champion to settle.

Record Spot

Melbourne Cup Win and a placing

Carbine	2nd	1889	1st	1890
The Grafter	2nd	1897	1st	1898
Lord Cardigan	1st	1903	2nd	1904
Westcourt	2nd	1915	1st	1917
Spearfelt	3rd	1924	1st	1926
Phar Lap	3rd	1929	1st	1930
Rising Fast	1st	1954	2nd	1955
Light Fingers	1st	1965	2nd	1966
Gold and Black	2nd	1976	1st	1977
Hyperno	3rd	1977	1st	1979
Empire Rose	2nd	1987	1st	1988
Vintage Crop	1st	1993	3rd	1995
Doriemus	1st	1995	2nd	1997
Fiorente	2nd	2012	1st	2013

Did You Know?

Fourteen horses have won the Melbourne Cup either before or after running a placing in the great race. Most have improved on a previous placing, most noticeably Carbine (1889–90) and most recently Fiorente (2012–2013), showing the championship qualities needed to win the Cup for their connections.

On three occasions, the Cup winner has returned a year later only to run second in the race – Lord Cardigan (1903-04), Rising Fast (1954–55) and Light Fingers (1965–66). On two other occasions, there has been a gap of two years between an unsuccessful Cup defence – Vintage Crop (1993 and 1995) and Doriemus (1995 and 1997).

Lord Cardigan
(1903)

L ord Cardigan is one of the more underrated Melbourne Cup winners, having denied the champion mare Wakeful a win in the 1903 Cup in what was to be her final race. In the 1903 Cup, three-year-old Lord Cardigan carried 6st 9lb (42kg) to Wakefield's massive 10st (63.5kg), and beat the mare by only three-quarters of a length. However, Lord Cardigan already had a victory over the mare in the Randwick Plate (by 6 lengths) and had run second to Wakeful in the Melbourne Stakes.

Lord Cardigan went on to win the 1904 Sydney Cup before having another tilt at Melbourne Cup. After running second in the Melbourne Stakes on the Saturday, Lord Nolan ran the seven-year-old mare Acrasia to three-quarters of a length carrying 9st 6lb (60kg). On the Saturday after the Melbourne Cup Lord Cardigan died from 'a strangulation of the intestines' thought to have been a result of over-exertion in the race.

Record Spot

Fillies and Mares

1876	Briseis (f)
1895	Auraria (f)
1904	Acrasia
1921	Sister Olive (f)
1939	Rivette
1945	Rainbird
1956	Evening Peal
1960	Hi Jinx
1965	Light Fingers
1988	Empire Rose
1991	Let's Elope
1998	Jezabeel
2001	Ethereal
2003	Makybe Diva
2004	Makybe Diva
2005	Makybe Diva

THE MELBORNE CUP 1904 "ACRASIA"   HARVIE & SUTCLIFFE

Did You Know?

Fillies and mares have won just 16 Melbourne Cups, with mares comprising just 8.4%
of Cup winners. It took 44 years for a mare to break through for a win (fillies had
already won two Melbourne Cups) when the seven-year-old Acrasia held off Lord
Nolan to win the 1904 Melbourne Cup. It was another 25 years before Rivette saluted
(Sister Olive won the Cup in 1921 as a three-year-old), with mares going on to have a
fair record in the race with five wins in the next 26 years.

It takes a mighty mare to win the Melbourne Cup, and Empire Rose (1988), Let's
Elope (1991), Ethereal (2001) and Makybe Diva (2003–05) are among the greatest in
the race's history. It's ironic that the old adage 'a good horse will beat a good mare' has
often held true when it comes to the Melbourne Cup, but a mare (Makybe Diva) holds
the record for most Cup wins.

**Above: In 1904 Acrasia became the first mare to win the Melbourne Cup,
defeating the previous year's winner Lord Nolan.**

Record Spot

Caulfield Cup – Melbourne Cup

1906	Poseidon	1982	Gurner's Lane
1937	The Trump	1991	Let's Elope
1939	Rivette	1995	Doriemus
1954	Rising Fast	1997	Might and Power
1962	Even Stevens	2001	Ethereal
1966	Galilee		

Did You Know?

The Caulfield Cup remains the best guide to Melbourne Cup success, although just 11 horses have won the big Cups double (about 7%). Most trainers use the Caulfield Cup (2400m) as a vital lead up to the race just over two weeks later, with punters comparing weights and how each respective horse finishes off their race as a guide to finding the Cup winner.

Horses to have won the Caulfield Cup after their Melbourne Cup success are Poseidon (1906 and 1907), Skipton (1941 and 1943), Rising Fast (1954 and 1955), Viewed (2008 and 2009) and Dunaden (2011 and 2012).

Interestingly, Doriemus not only won the double in 1995, but two years later was runner-up to bold front-runner Might and Power in both races. Rising Fast almost captured the Cups double twice, but went down to the lightly weighted Toparoa in the 1955 Melbourne Cup after winning his second successive Caulfield Cup that year.

Poseidon
(1906)

Poseidon (Positano GB – Jacinth) ranks as one of the greatest three-year-olds in Australian turf history. After a moderate two-year season (one win from six starts), Poseidon won the AJC Derby, Caulfield Cup, VRC Derby and Melbourne Cup. In eight runs during the Spring, Poseidon's only defeat was in the AJC Metropolitan where it ran second to the mare Solution, which would later start as favourite in the Melbourne Cup.

Poseidon not only became the first horse to capture the Caulfield Cup–Melbourne Cup double, but was also a dual Derby winner. Poseidon started at 4/1 and beat another good three-year-old in Antonius by one and a half lengths. Trained by Ike Earnshaw and ridden by Tom Clayton in all his career starts, Poseidon won 11 of 14 starts as three-year-old including the AJC and VRC St. Legers.

Poseidon won a second Caulfield Cup in 1907 but failed in the Melbourne Cup and was retired to stud the following year. Trainer Ike Earnshaw celebrated a second win in the race with the New Zealand-bred Apologue, which started 3/1 favourite in the 1908 Cup.

History Spot
Prince Foote
(1909)

Prince Foote won a 'clean sweep' of the three-year-old classics in 1909–10 – both St. Legers and the Champion Stakes as well as the 1909 Melbourne Cup. Considered one of the greatest colts in Australian racing history, Prince Foote won classic races at two, three and four before being retired to stud after a disappointing Spring campaign as a five-year-old.

Prince Foote started at 4/1 equal favourite (with Sydney Cup winner Trafalgar) in the 1909 Melbourne Cup and defeated the 1908 VRC Derby winner Alawa (ridden by Bobby Lewis) by three lengths. Aberdeen ran third at 100/1, just ahead of Trafalgar in fourth place.

A silver centrepiece was awarded to the owners of Prince Foote, which was ridden by Bill 'Midge' McLachlan, the great-grandfather of future five-time Cup winning trainer Lee Freedman.

Did You Know?

Only two foreign bred horses won the Melbourne Cup in just over a century – Comedy King (1910) and Backwood (1924) – before Beldale Ball (1980) became the first of three USA-bred horses to win the Cup in the 1980s. Since the year 2000, northern hemisphere-bred horses won 10 of the 16 Melbourne Cups contested.

Four other Cup winners post-2000 were bred in New Zealand, leaving only two Australian-bred horses to win the race since the turn of the century – Viewed (Sadler's Wells – Lover's Knot) in 2008 and Shocking (Street Cry – Maria Di Castiglia) in 2009.

Record Spot

Internationally-bred winners, other than NZ

1910	Comedy King (England)
1924	Backwood (England)
1980	Beldale Ball (USA)
1986	At Talaq (USA)
1990	Kingston Rule (USA)
1993	Vintage Crop (England) *
1994	Jeune (England)
2002	Media Puzzle (USA) *
2003-05	Makybe Diva (England)
2006	Delta Blues (Japan) *
2010	Americain (USA) *
2011	Dunaden (France) *
2012	Green Moon (Ireland)
2013	Fiorente (Ireland)
2014	Protectionist (Germany) *

* Internationally-trained

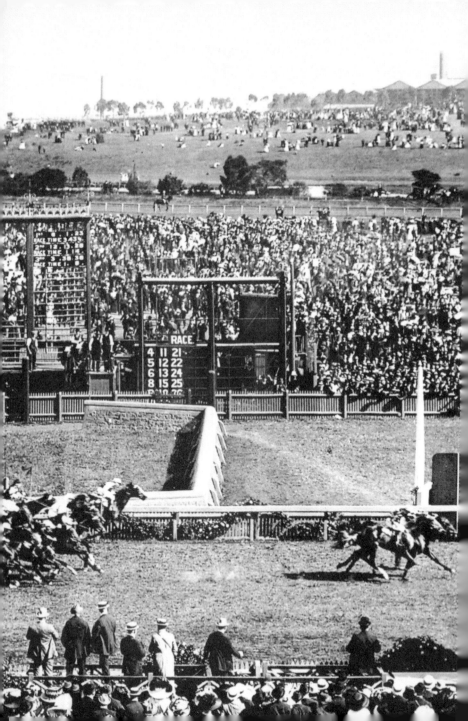

Comedy King
(1910)

English-bred Comedy King and its mother Tragedy Queen were imported to Australia by high profile bookmaker Sol Green in 1908. The colt was sired by Persimmon, the English Derby winner owned by King Edward VII. Comedy King did not race as a two-year-old but won the Futurity Stakes as his second race start before going for a spell and being aimed at the 1910 Melbourne Cup.

After winning the Spring Stakes at Randwick on 1 October 1910, Comedy King took the Cup at its next start, carrying 7st 11lb (49kg) and starting at 10/1. Runner-up Trafalgar was described as 'a perfect specimen of a horse' and became an Australian favourite, eventually winning 23 races, but he never beat Comedy King in eight races. It was the second successive victory for jockey Bill McLachlan, following the win of Prince Foote in 1909.

Comedy King was retired to Mr Green's Shipley Stud, before the stock was dispersed in 1918. At stud, Comedy King sired future Cup winners Artilleryman (1919) and King Ingoda (1922), as well as Shadow King (four placings in 1930–33). The 50th Melbourne Cup featured the only silver cup ever presented and the trophy now sits in the National Sports Museum.

Opposite: English import Comedy King holds off the aptly named Trafalgar to win the 1910 Melbourne Cup.

Record Spot

Internationally trained winners

1916	Sasanof (New Zealand)	1983	Kiwi (New Zealand)
1929	Nightmarch (New Zealand)	1988	Empire Rose (New Zealand)
1936	Wotan (New Zealand)	1993	Vintage Crop (Ireland*)
1938	Catalogue (New Zealand)	1998	Jezabeel (New Zealand)
1952	Dalray (New Zealand)	2000	Brew (New Zealand)
1954	Rising Fast (New Zealand)	2001	Ethereal (New Zealand)
1960	Hi Jinx (New Zealand)	2002	Media Puzzle (Ireland*)
1962	Even Stevens (New Zealand)	2006	Delta Blues (Japan)
1964	Polo Prince (New Zealand)	2010	Americain (France)
1970	Baghdad Note (New Zealand)	2011	Dunaden (France)
1971	Silver Knight (New Zealand)	2014	Protectionist (Germany)
1976	Van der Hum (New Zealand)		

*both by Irish trainer Dermot Weld

Did You Know?

Internationally-trained horses came entirely from New Zealand before the VRC started to actively promote the Melbourne Cup to northern hemisphere trainers and owners in the 1990s. In 1916 Sasanoff, trained by Murray Hobbs, was the first New Zealand-trained horse to win the Melbourne Cup with another fifteen Kiwi-trained horses tasting success.

Since the turn of this century, international trainers have won seven of the sixteen Cups decided. Dermot O'Brien (Ireland) became the first international trainer to win two Melbourne Cups in 2002 after Media Puzzle emulated the deeds of 1993 winner Vintage Crop.

History Spot

Sasanof
(1916)

Sasanof was the first New Zealand-bred, owned and trained horse to the win the Melbourne Cup. Other Cup winners had been bred in New Zealand (Martini-Henri and Carbine), and Apologue was bred and owned in New Zealand (but trained by Sydney's Ike Earnshaw), but the son of Martian (NZ) was trained by Murray Hobbs, a long-time owner-trainer in Auckland.

A star two-year-old in his homeland, Sasanof won the AJC Chelmsford Stakes and the AJC Spring Stakes before running a good third in the Caulfield Cup. Having bypassed the classic three-year-old races, Sasanof was given just 6st 12lb (43.5kg) in the 1916 Melbourne Cup.

In 1916, the Cup was postponed until the following Thursday after heavy rain, which certainly suited the New Zealanders. Ridden by F.Foley and starting at 12/1, Sasanof relegated the great Bobby Lewis to another minor prize on runner-up Shepherd King, the Caulfield Cup winner, which started 4/1 favourite. St. Spasa ran third at 50/1 to make it a clean sweep for the 'S' horses.

Sasanof proved his class by returning home and winning the ARC Great Northern Derby (1917), CJC New Zealand Cup (1918), the WRC Trentham Gold Cup (1919) and two Awapuni Gold Cups (1919 and 1921).

WESTCOURT. (JOCKEY W H. McLACHLAN)

History Spot

Artilleryman
(1919)

Artilleryman, by champion sire Comedy King (GB) out of the New Zealand mare Cross Battery, was bred by Sol Green at Shipley Stud and foaled in 1916. The three-year-old colt famously dead-heated with Richmond Main in the 1919 AJC Derby before running second to that horse in the VRC Derby at 5/4.

With Bobby Lewis in the saddle, Artilleryman was sent out a 10/1 chance in the Cup, shading Richmond Main at 11/1. English import Lucknow, which had won the Caulfield Cup, was the 6/1 favourite in the race. Artilleryman scored the easiest win since Newhaven, beating Richmond Main by 6 lengths in race record time. The Sydney colt then finished the carnival by taking out the CB Fisher Plate at 3/1 on.

Artilleryman won five successive races in the Autumn before being sensationally beaten in the AJC St Leger at 12/1 on. A failure in Poitrel's Sydney Cup win in 1920 confirmed something was amiss with the colt. Tragically, Artilleryman died from lymphatic cancer before the end of his three-year-old season.

Did You Know?

The three-handled 'loving cup' was awarded to the connections of Artilleryman in 1919. Manufactured by Drummonds Jewellers and handmade by James W. Steeth and Son, the Cup was valued at £150 and weighed just over 2kg. Today, that iconic Cup weighs almost 4kg and is valued at more than $175,000

Record Spot

Winning Barriers since 1924*

1	5	(Prince of Penzance 2015)	15	1	(Silver Knight 1971)
2	2	(Might and Power 1997)	16	3	(Jezabeel 1998)
3	3	(Media Puzzle 2002)	17	4	(At Talaq 1986)
4	4	(Kensei 1987)	18	0	(no winner)
5	8	(Fiorente 2013)	19	5	(Red Handed 1967)
6	5	(Light Fingers 1965)	20	2	(Empire Rose 1988)
7	2	(Makybe Diva 2004)	21	3	(Rogan Josh 1999)
8	5	(Viewed 2008)	22	4	(Shocking 2009)
9	2	(Just a Dash 1981)	23	2	(Van der Hum 1976)
10	7	(Protectionist 2014)	24	3	(Gala Supreme 1973)
11	7	(Protectionist 2014)	25	2	(Peter Pan 1934)
12	2	(Foxzami 1949)	26	0	(no winner)
13	4	(Dunaden 2011)	27	1	(Trivalve 1927)
14	6	(Makybe Diva 2005)			

* Year barrier positions were introduced

Did You Know?

When the Melbourne Cup began in the 1860s, horses started the race with a 'standing start'. The horses would line up in any order and when the starter dropped his flag the horses and their jockeys were off! Often horses would miss the start altogether.

Strand starts were introduced to Flemington in 1894. A tape was stretched across the width of the track to keep the horses in line and to ensure no horse received an advantage. The tape would be raised and the horses would be on their way ... unfortunately, as in the case of Cup favourite Eurythmic in 1921, horses often got their heads up over the tape, and when it was raised mayhem would ensue. And still, others missed the start.

In the 1920s, horses were allocated barrier positions for their races and had to stand in these positons at the starting tape. The first Cup with designated starting positions was in 1924, won by the imported Backwood which started in barrier 'lucky' seven. In the ensuing decades, barrier stands were developed which allowed groups of horses to stand beside each other and not crowd each other for room, but this was far from perfect.

In the 1958 Cup, won by Baystone, horses commenced from individual starting gates for the first time. The stalls were not perfect – they constricted larger horses and legs were often caught in the frame – but they afforded all horses an even chance of a fair start.

Inside barriers are a slight advantage in the Melbourne Cup with 52 winners coming from inside barriers 1/12 (56.5%) to 40 winners from 'outside' barriers.

In almost 100 years of designated starting positions, no horse has won the Cup from barrier 18.

Record Spot

Successful Trainers

4 wins	James Scobie:	
	Clean Sweep (1900)	King Ingoda (1922)
	Bitalli (1923)	Trivalve (1927)

Trainer (and former jockey) James Scobie (1860–1940) won four Melbourne Cups between 1900 and 1927. A measure of his skill was Bitalli's win in the 1923 Melbourne Cup 'first up' after a three-month break. Trivalve (1927), which was also a dual Derby winner, was bred at Melton Stud where Scobie was non-resident manager for clients Rupert and Ernest Clarke.

Stand By (1924) was also an unlucky second to Backwood, which would have given Scobie a trio of Cup wins after the success of King Ingoda (1922) and Bitalli (1923). Piastre (1912) was originally trained by Scobie but was transferred to Richard O'Connor in Sydney prior to its Cup success.

Did You Know?

The first radio broadcast of the Melbourne Cup was made by the Australian Broadcasting Company in 1925. The winner was the aptly named Windbag.

After the 1933 Melbourne Cup, won by Hall Mark, film of the race was flown to Sydney by famed aviator Charles Kingsford Smith, where it was shown later that night to enraptured audiences.

The first televised Melbourne Cup was in 1957, won by Straight Draw, a year after TV started in Australia.

Windbag
(1925)

Windbag (Magpie GB – Charleville NZ) was an exceptionally talented three-year-old, but injury ruled the star colt out of the 1924 Spring Carnival. The following Autumn, Windbag won the AJC St. Leger before running second in the Sydney Cup. Windbag then won seven successive races into its four-year-old season. A third in the Melbourne Stakes to WFA star Pelliewinkle saw Windbag go out a firm second favourite in the 1925 Melbourne Cup.

The undoubted star that year, however, was the three-year-old Manfred, which had won the AJC Derby (after missing the start by 100 metres), the WS Cox Plate and the VRC Derby (by 12 lengths) leading into the Melbourne Cup. Carrying 7st 8lb (48kg), Manfred started 7/4 favourite in the Cup, but Windbag gave away weight (carrying 9st 2lb or 58kg) and won by half a length, with Pelliewinkle third. The 1925 Melbourne Cup was a class race; first and second carried 2lb (1kg) over weight-for-age and set a new race record in the process.

Record Spot

Cox Plate – Melbourne Cup

1929	Nightmarch
1930	Phar Lap
1954	Rising Fast
1996	Saintly
2005	Makybe Diva

Did You Know?

The WS Cox Plate (2040m) is Australia's second richest WFA race, run at Mooney Valley Racecourse two weeks and three days before the Melbourne Cup. Many racing purists view this race as Australia's premier racing event, but traditionally it did not have a huge bearing on the Melbourne Cup. Today, however, it is the preferred lead-up race under testing WFA conditions on a turning track for local international trainers. It's also worth $3,000,000, which is a lot of cabbage!

Only five horses have completed the Cox Plate–Melbourne Cup double, and only two in the past 20 years, but they are all champions.

Nightmarch
(1929)

The 1929 Melbourne Cup is the story of two horses, both by the sire Night Raid (GB) and both from New Zealand. The first, foaled in 1925 and named Nightmarch, was a New Zealand Derby winner which came to Australia in the Spring of 1929 and captured the Epsom Handicap (1600m) and Cox Plate (2040m) on the way to the Melbourne Cup.

The other, foaled in 1926 and named Phar Lap, won four races in succession including the AJC and VRC Derbies, and was the shortest priced favourite ever to start in a Melbourne Cup. Although the gelding only had 7st 6lb (47kg) in the Cup, it refused to settle for jockey Bobby Lewis and faded to third after trying to lead all the way.

Ridden by his usual New Zealand rider Roy Reed, Nightmarch swept past Phar Lap to win by three lengths, with fellow Kiwi Paquito (ridden by future trainer Maurice McCarten) grabbing second place by a length. Nightmarch carried the good horse's weight of 9st 2lb (58kg), or 2lb (1kg) over weight for age, but he was no match for Phar Lap in the 1930–31 season and returned home to New Zealand to win the CJC New Zealand Cup.

Record Spot

Did You Know?

Phar Lap remains the only horse to be sent out at odds on, meaning punters had to stake more money than they actually won (e.g. 11/8 on means for every $11 dollars spent, a punter will win only $8 for a total return of $19). Phar Lap also held the previous short odds record when it was sent out an even money favourite in the 1929 Cup (meaning, for every $1 spent a punter won a $1), but only ran third.

Favourites or co-favourites have won of 33 of 155 Melbourne Cups, 21% or about 1 in 5 Cups. Since 2000, three favourites have won the Cup – Makybe Diva in 2004 ($3.60) and 2005 ($4.40), and Fiorente in 2013 ($7).

Following spread: Phar Lap easily wins the 1930 Melbourne Cup, to the delight of the Depression-era crowd.

Phar Lap
(1930)

Entire books have been written about Phar Lap, 'The Red Terror', and his win in the 1930 Melbourne Cup, so what can be added in one or two paragraphs that could possibly shed any new light on the champion? The stats are impressive. Phar Lap won 37 of his 51 starts, including 14 straight races in his four-year-old season, and amassed a record £66,738 in prize money.

Phar Lap won the Cox Plate–Melbourne Stakes double before carrying 9st 12lb (62.5kg) to an effortless 3 length win over Second Wind and Shadow King in the 1930 Melbourne Cup. In doing so, the chestnut gelding started the shortest priced favourite in Cup history, and landed some huge bets for those canny punters who coupled Phar Lap with Amounis in the Caulfield Cup. Trainer Harry Telford backed the horse up on the Thursday and Saturday of Cup week to win four races in eight days.

In many instances, there was no betting on the race because Phar Lap was deemed unbeatable at WFA. The handicapper finally beat him, however, allotting him a record 10st10lb (68kg) in the 1931 Melbourne Cup. Starting a 3/1 favourite, Phar Lap raced like a tired horse and finished unplaced behind White Nose and the unlucky Shadow King.

With nowhere else to turn, Phar Lap's American owner Dave Davies sent the champion to America to race, where he won the Agua Caliente before succumbing to travel sickness in April 1932. Some said Phar Lap was poisoned, others said he was just worn out ... a dream destroyed.

Record Spot

Multiple Cup Placings

4 placings	Shadow King (1930, 1931, 1933)
3 placings	Sarcherie (1934, 1935, 1937)
	Red Cadeaux (2011, 2013, 2014)
2 placings	Mormon (1861, 1862)
	Rose of Denmark (1863, 1864)
	Exile (1866, 1867)
	Dagworth (1872, 1873)
	Sweetmeat (1879, 1881)
	Commotion (1883, 1884)
	Trenton (1885, 1886)
	Silvermine (1886, 1887)
	Maikai (1939, 1940)
	Ilumquh (1960, 1963)
	Noble Comment (1982, 1983)
	Persian Punch (1998, 2001)

Did You Know?

Shadow King holds the record for most placings in the Melbourne Cup without winning – four placings in consecutive years (1930–33) – but we shouldn't forget the luckless Sarcherie and Red Cadeaux. The latter horse became a crowd favourite with a trio of Cup seconds (the gelding was unplaced in the 2012 and 2015 Cups), while the mare Sarcherie finished second to Peter Pan in 1934, second to Marabou in 1935 and was a nose third to The Trump two years later in 1937.

Eleven horses have been placed twice in a Melbourne Cup without winning, commencing with Mormon in 1861–62 which was denied its place in history by the immortal Archer. Illumquh had a three-year gap between its placings, from 1960 and 1963, as did the import Persian Punch (1998 and 2001). Spare a thought for the George Hanlon-trained Noble Comment. Having beaten all but Gurner's Lane and Kingston Town in an epic 1982 Cup, Noble Comment was being hailed the winner in 1983 just as Kiwi swept down the outside to victory.

History Spot

Peter Pan
(1932 and 1934)

It is ironic that the death of Phar Lap in 1932 would also see a new star heralded in Australian racing. Peter Pan, an impressive-looking chestnut colt trained in Sydney by Frank McGrath, burst into Melbourne Cup calculations win a win the AJC Derby. Peter Pan ran a good fourth in the Caulfield Cup before victory in the Melbourne Stakes saw the colt sent out a 4/1 favourite on Cup Day. Peter Pan beat Yarramba by a neck, with Shadow King two lengths away in third place.

Australia had a new racing star to cheer, but injury ruled Peter Pan out of the 1933 Melbourne Cup carnival. A year later, the then five-year-old stallion won a second Melbourne Stakes but drifted to 14/1 for the Cup given it had to carry 9st 10lb (61.5kg) on a heavy track. Peter Pan sailed through the going to win by three lengths, to become the second horse to win two Melbourne Cups and the only horse to win non-consecutive Melbourne Cups.

Peter Pan returned to racing in 1935 and reeled off eight straight wins, but a third Melbourne Cup (carrying 10st 6lb or 66kg) was beyond him and he was unplaced. Retired to stud, his progeny Precept (1943 VRC Derby) and Peter (second in the 1944 Melbourne Cup) inherited but a slither of Peter Pan's racing ability.

Opposite: Dual Melbourne Cup winner Peter Pan, ridden by Phar Lap's regular Australian rider Jim Pike.

The Trump
(1937)

The Trump, the son of Manfred, struck a purple patch of form in the Spring of 1937 after being gelded and having his problematic knees pin-fired. Winning five successive races, including the Toorak Handicap (1600m), Caulfield Cup (2400m) and Mackinnon Stakes (2000m) leading into the Melbourne Cup, not usurpingly The Trump started 11/2 favourite in the Cup before becoming the first horse since Poseidon (1906) to win the 'big Cups' double.

The Trump was trained by Stan Reid and owned by Darcy Eccles, the owner of Melbourne Cup runners up The Cypher (1922) and Yarramba (1932). The unsung hero of the gelding's Cup win was veterinarian S.Wood, who treated The Trump's suspect knees throughout his Autumn campaign. Few believed the small sprinter could stay, let alone win the Caulfield–Melbourne Cups double, but The Trump proved everyone wrong.

The Trump won only one more race, over 1200m the following August, and ran last in the 1938 Melbourne Cup. As a hardy gelding, The Trump's connections persevered towards the 1939 Melbourne Cup, but the gelding broke down during the race and was retired to a paddock.

Record Spot

Age of Melbourne Cup Winners			
	3 Years	23	(Skipton 1941)
	4 Years	43	(Shocking 2009)
	5 Years	44	(Protectionist 2014)
	6 Years	33	(Prince of Penzance 2015)
	7 Years	10	(Makybe Diva 2005)
	8 Years	2	(Catalogue 1938)

Did You Know?

Catalogue is one of only two eight-year-olds to win the Melbourne Cup, the other being Toryboy (1865). Catalogue was actually trained by Mrs. A. McDonald in New Zealand, but at the time, women could not be registered as trainers in Australia, and her husband's name was substituted as the trainer.

History Spot

Rivette
(1939)

In 1939 Rivette became the first mare to win the Caulfield Cup–Melbourne Cup double. Unfashionably bred by owner-trainer Harry Bamber, the former World War I horseman scraped together enough money during the Depression years to send his broodmare Riv to by served by Ronsard (GB). In 1938, Bamber set Rivette for the Cups double, and backed her to win £15,000. Unfortunately, Rivette cracked her fetlock in training and had to be scratched for the Autumn. A year later, Rivette won three races in succession before capturing the Caulfield Cup. Rivette was penalised 10lb (4.5kg) for the Melbourne Cup, requiring her to still carry the luxury weight of 7st 9lb (48.5kg) for a six-year-old mare.

Rivette ousted Mosaic as race favourite on the heavy Flemington track, starting at 5/1 and beating Maikal by a half-length. There was scare for jockey Teddy Preston when a horse flashed up on his inside in the run to the finishing post and quickly overtook him. For a moment, Preston thought the Cup was lost, but then it became clear that it was the riderless Ortelle's Star which had dumped its jockey when The Trump broke down in front of them.

Harry Bamber, who won £2,000 on his mare winning the double, announced Rivette's retirement after the Melbourne Cup. His little mare had set him up for life.

Opposite: Rivette, the first mare to win the Caulfield Cup–Melbourne Cup double. Jockey Teddy Preston received a scare when the riderless Ortelle's Star surged past him close to the finishing post.

Record Spot

Sex	
Entires	70 (Protectionist 2014)
Geldings	52 (Prince of Penzance 2015)
Colts	20 (Skipton 1941)
Mares	13 (Makybe Diva 2005)
Fillies	3 (Sister Olive 1921)

Did You Know?

Three-year-olds had a great record in the Melbourne Cup in the first half of the race's history, with 23 colts and fillies successful from 1861 to 1941 (32.3%). Many colts would use the VRC Derby, held three days before the Cup, as an indication to whether they could take on the rigours of a two-mile handicap against the older horses. Aiding their task was the weight-for-age scale where three-year-olds would carry around 7 stone 7lb (47.5kg), although this has since been changed to a minimum 50kg.

Since Skipton completed the VRC Derby–Melbourne Cup double in 1941, however, no three-year-old has been successful in the Cup. In fact, very few even start in a Cup. Comic Court ran third in 1948 before retuning to win the Cup two years later. Prince Darius, the Derby runner-up to Tulloch, chased home Straight Draw in 1957. Clear Prince (3rd in 1970) and Nothin' Leica Dane (2nd in 1995) were also placed, and for a while the VRC tried to encourage Derby winners to back up by granting them automatic entry into the Cup. Arena (1998) took up that challenge but was unplaced behind Jezabeel.

Skipton
(1941)

Skipton, a son of 1935 Cup winner Marabou, was the last three-year-old colt to win the Melbourne Cup and the last to win the VRC Derby–Melbourne Cup double. Trained by former New Zealander Jack Fryer, the trainer of 1936 Cup winner Wotan, Skipton was ridden by Fryer's son-in-law, Norman Creighton, in its Derby success but Creighton couldn't make the three-year-old's weight for the Cup.

Champion Sydney jockey Billy Cook took the ride on Skipton and carrying 7st 7lb (47.5kg) the colt won easily after being near last mid race. Son of Aurous was second, with New Zealand champion Beau Vite third. A multiple Cup and Derby winner in his homeland, and a dual Cox Plate and Mackinnon Stakes winner (1940–41) in Australia, Beau Vite had run 4th to Old Rowley in the 1940 Cup and had to settle for a minor placing in 1941.

Did You Know?

Billy Cook (1910–1985) won two Melbourne Cups – on Skipton in 1941 and Rainbird in 1945. Four decades later, his son Peter Cook (born 1950) won two Melbourne Cups – on Just a Dash (1981) and Black Knight (1984). They remain the only father and son jockey combination to win the Melbourne Cup.

2 Nov 1942

MELBOURNE CUP

WIN AND PLACE.
Place only quarter of odds.

14	Amazed	6	10	50	Phocion *2nd*	7	5
66	Colonus	7	2	100	Prairiedale	7	9
5	Dark Felt	7	7	33	Ronolive	6	13
50	Grain Trader	7	3	100	Royal Peter	7	5
5	Great Britain	7	6	33	Similar	7	7
10	Gusher	7	7	5	Skipton	9	2
25	Heart's Desire *3rd*	7	2	16	Son of Aurous	7	3
50	Hestia	7	7	20	Spearmain	8	2
33	Maikai	8	11	66	Throttle	7	4
100	Manawatu	6	7	7	Tranquil Star	9	3
20	Mercury Bay	7	0	33	Velocity	8	13
7	Pandect	8	13	50	Wilson	8	1
40	Pandini	6	10				

Won By 7 Lengths.

SUBJECT TO MARKET ALTERATION

Register All Letters containing Cash or P/Notes.

A rare bookmaker's card from the 1942 Melbourne Cup, with handwritten results. Note the winner Colonus is quoted at double his official starting price at the juicy odds of 66/1.

History Spot

Colonus
(1942)

From 1942 to 1944 the Melbourne Cup was run on Saturdays during the war years. The Derby was held on Saturday, November 14, with the Cup and the Oaks conducted the following Saturday. Described as the 'Austerity Melbourne Cup', no trophy was presented due to war-time restrictions. Instead, the winning prize money and a £200 war bond was awarded to the owner of winner, Colonus, Mr L.O. Menck. The wealthy businessman later approached the trophy's manufacturers to have a replica Cup made.

Apprentice jockey Harry McCloud took the four-year-old horse Colonus to the lead soon after the start and was never threatened, winning by seven lengths – the greatest winning margin since Archer in 1862. There were another five lengths between second and third. Colonus, which was trained as a sprinter in his early career, had won the Herbert Power Handicap in similar circumstances, but still started at the odds of 33/1 in the Cup.

Dark Felt started favourite in the 1942 Melbourne Cup at 9/2, but although the heavy conditions didn't suit the horse, it would only have to wait another twelve months to make amends.

History Spot

Rimfire
(1948)

The 1948 Melbourne Cup remains one of the most controversial on record. The lightly waited Rimfire, an 80/1 outsider, defeated the well-performed Dark Marne by half a head after a tense battle down the Flemington straight. The 'photo finish' had recently been installed at Flemington and when Rimfire's number was semaphored, many on course believed the photo must be wrong.

There has been a lot of conjecture over the years whether the photo finish was aligned correctly, but the truth is Rimfire did actually win the race.

Rimfire was ridden by sixteen-year-old apprentice Ray Neville, who was chosen because he could ride at the correct weight of 7st 2lb (45.4 kilograms). Trainer Stan Boyden didn't tell Neville he had been engaged for the horse until the morning of the race so the boy wouldn't lose any sleep.

Ray Neville outrode premier Sydney jockey Jack Thompson, then at the peak of his powers, who was fated never to win a Melbourne Cup. It was only Neville's ninth ever ride in a race and he never rode another winner.

Opposite: The controversial finish of the 1948 Melbourne Cup with Rimfire, ridden by 16-year-old apprentice Ray Neville, holding off the challenge of race favourite Dark Marne on the outside. A stride past the post, Dark Marne was in front but the photo told a different story.

History Spot

Comic Court
(1950)

Comic Court, trained by Jim Cummings the father of future 'Cups King' Bart Cummings, was South Australian born and bred. A star two-year-old in Adelaide, Comic Court won the VRC Derby and VRC St Leger as a three-year-old, and ran fourth to Rimfire in the 1948 Melbourne Cup.

Comic Court won eight races as a four-year-old, as well as placing in the Cox Plate and Caulfield Cup, but when he failed in the 1949 Melbourne Cup behind Foxzami, many doubted his ability to stay. The five-year-old stallion was troubled by a torn chest muscle in the Spring of 1950, and fell out of favour with punters with an unplaced run in the Caulfield Cup. But Jim Cummings never doubted the horses' ability to stay the two miles of the Melbourne Cup.

Even though Comic Court won the Mackinnon Stakes, it was sent out at 25/1 outsider for the 1950 Melbourne Cup. Jockey Jack Purtell preferred to ride Alister in the Cup, which many punters saw as an omen and backed the colt into 3/1 favouritism. Carrying 9st 5lb (59.5kg), under the riding of Adelaide jockey Pat Glennon, Comic Court led all the way to win by three lengths in race record time. Alister was unplaced.

Comic Court's strapper that day was Jim Cummings' 21-year-old son Bart.

Opposite: Comic Court careers away with the 1950 Melbourne Cup.

History Spot

Delta
(1951)

Delta was one of the most consistent performers to win the Melbourne Cup, being a star at three, four and five years of age. A Cox Plate-VRC Derby winner at three, the Maurice McCarten-trained colt started 6/1 favourite in running fifth in Foxzami's 1949 Melbourne Cup carrying 7st 7lb (47.5kg). The following year, Delta won the VRC St Leger-VRC King's Plate double, but his 1950s Melbourne Cup campaign was aborted and the horse spelled until the following Spring.

It was in Delta's five-year-old season he proved his class, winning 11 of his 14 starts. Delta won the AJC Metropolitan before capturing the 1951 Mackinnon Stakes. Allotted top weight of 9st 5lb (59kg) in the Melbourne Cup, Delta started at 10/1 with punters putting their faith in favourite Morse Code (Jack Thompson). Unfortunately, Morse Code fell in the race and under the hard riding of Neville Sellwood, Delta overhauled 7/1 chance Akbar to win the Cup by three quarters of a length. Delta had beaten Akbar in the Mackinnon Stakes the previous Saturday, so the form had certainly held up.

Delta became the first horse since Tim Whiffler (1867) to win the Metropolitan Handicap–Melbourne Cup double, and returned in the Autumn to win six successive WFA races in before an unplaced run in the 1952 Melbourne Cup. He was retired to stud after chipping a sesamoid bone preparing for another title at the Melbourne Cup but, unlike his turf career, was a relative failure.

History Spot

Dalray
(1952)

After a slow start in his native New Zealand, Dalray crossed the Tasman at the end of his three-year-old year and showed his potential with a good second in the 1952 Sydney Cup. Dalray was obviously weighted to his potential in the 1952 Melbourne Cup when the four-year-old was given 9st 6lb (60kg) – 6lb (2.7kg) over weight for age – before being penalised another 2lb (1kg) after winning the AJC Metropolitan. The only four-year-old to carry more weight in a Cup was Phar Lap.

Trained by Clarrie McCarthy, Dalray won the Mackinnon Stakes, which saw him form into 5/1 favouritism for the Cup. Dalray was ridden by Melbourne hoop Bill Williamson in the Mackinnon Stakes, replacing the horse's regular rider Ken Nutall. Nutall was actually dressing into Dalray's colours on race day when volatile owner Mr Cyril Neville told him he was being replaced as the horse's jockey. Nutall immediately dressed and flew straight home to New Zealand.

Ridden a patient race by Williamson, Dalray wore down 200/1 outsider Welkie Sun to win the Cup by a half-length, with fellow New Zealander Reformed back in third place. Neville reportedly won £50,000 on the win, and divided the prize money (£9,800) between his trainer and jockey. He also paid former jockey Ken Nutall the full £513 winner's fee and donated £1000 to charity.

Record Spot

Moonee Valley Cup – Melbourne Cup

1900	Clean Sweep
1905	Blue Spec
1953	Wodalla
1990	Kingston Rule

Did You Know?

The Mooney Valley Cup is a 2500m race with set weights and penalty conditions conducted on Cox Plate Day, 10 days before the Melbourne Cup. First run in 1883, it has traditionally been a poor guide to Melbourne Cup success with only four winners going on to capture the Cup.

Clean Sweep (1900) and Blue Spec (1905) completed the double at the turn of the last century, but it wasn't until 1953 when Wodalla greeted the judge, that another Mooney Valley Cup winner went on to win the Melbourne Cup. From 1976 to 1979, the Mooney Valley Cup was shifted to the Spring with The Governor's Stakes substituted as a Melbourne Cup lead up.

The only Mooney Valley Cup winner to go on and capture the Melbourne Cup in the years since was Kingston Rule in 1990, although 2015 runner-up Prince of Penzance won the Melbourne Cup in a boil-over at 100/1.

Opposite: Mooney Valley Cup winner Wodalla, ridden by the great Jack Purtell, returns to scale after winning the 1953 Melbourne Cup.

NEW ZEALAND
HOOF BEATS

Rising Fast's
Melbourne and Caulfield Cup

Rising Fast
(1954)

In 1954, New Zealand bred Rising Fast became the first horse to complete the Caulfield Cup–Cox Plate–Melbourne Cup treble. In an incredible run of seven straight wins, Rising Fast also captured the Feehan Stakes, Turnbull Stakes, Caulfield Stakes and Mackinnon Stakes on the way to the historic treble, and then backed up the following Saturday to win the CB Fisher Plate.

Rising Fast was ridden by Jack Purtell (who had won the Cup the previous year on Wodalla) in 1954 after the horse's regular rider Bill Williamson was injured in a fall on Caulfield Cup day. Carrying 9st 5lb (59.5kg), Rising Fast beat Hellion by one and a quarter lengths, with 200/1 roughie Gay Hellios third.

The following year, Rising Fast attempted to achieve a historic double under the guidance of Australian trainer Fred Hoystead, following the suspension of New Zealand trainer Ivan Tucker. Rising Fast won the Caulfield Cup and Mackinnon Stakes for a second time, but was beaten by the Tommy Smith-trained lightweight Toparoa in a rain-affected 1955 Melbourne Cup.

Rising Fast carried 10st (63.5kg) to Toparoa's 7st 8lb (48kg), with Sir William a distant third. Toparoa's jockey Neville Sellwood was later suspended for two months for causing interference to the 2/1 favourite but Rising Fast's run had ended short of the winning post and his jockey declined to protest.

History Spot

Evening Peal
(1956)

As Australia prepared for the Melbourne Olympics in November 1956, four-year-old mare Evening Peal won the Melbourne Cup, denying the champion Redcraze victory in the race.

Originally trained by Sid Brown in New Zealand, Redcraze transferred to Tommy Smith in Sydney and won the Brisbane Cup-Metropolitan Handicap double that year. Redcraze then set a weight carrying record of 9st 13lb (63kg) in winning the 1956 Caulfield Cup and started a short 7/4 favourite in the Melbourne Cup.

Carrying 10st 3lb (65kg) in the Cup, the most weight since Phar Lap in 1931, Redcraze was gallant in defeat in going down to Evening Peal. The mare had won the VRC Oaks the previous year and became the first Oaks winner to win the Cup as an older mare. Another grand champion competed in that race as well. Rising Fast had already won a Cup, and run second in 1955, but under the steadier of 10st 2lb (64.5kg), the veteran champ could only fifth in 1956.

Redcraze later started favourite in the 1957 Melbourne Cup too, but was unplaced after playing a minor role in the drama concerning his illustrious stablemate Tulloch.

Did You Know?

Champion three-year-old Tulloch had the 1957 Melbourne Cup at his mercy. A star two-year-old which battled the great Todman in his debut season, Tulloch developed into a once in a lifetime horse for his elderly owner Ted Haley and trainer Tommy Smith. In the Spring of 1957, Tulloch won six successive races, including the AJC and VRC Derbies and the Caulfield Guineas-Caulfield Cup double, and appeared to have the Melbourne Cup at his mercy.

On October 20, after Tulloch's record win as 6/4 on favourite in the Caulfield Cup, Tommy Smith scratched Tulloch from the Melbourne Cup. Ted Haley had publicly stated it was too much to ask of the colt to run in a two-mile race against the older horses and didn't want to 'break his heart'. Tulloch was given 8st 10lb (55.5kg, or 7.5kg over WFA) for the Cup, but in the end it was Smith's decision to scratch the horse.

Smith, of course, had Redcraze ready for the big race and although Tulloch looked unbeatable after defeating Prince Darius in the VRC Derby by eight lengths, what was done was done.

How far would Tulloch have won by? Straight Draw, the Metropolitan Handicap winner, beat Prince Darius by a neck carrying 8st 5lb (53kg). Tulloch won the CB Fisher Plate on the final day of the carnival at 8/1 on. The colt later went amiss, and did not come back to racing until he was a five-year-old in 1960.

Record Spot

Metropolitan Hcp – Melbourne Cup

1867	Tim Whiffler
1951	Delta
1952	Dalray
1957	Straight Draw
1959	Macdougall

Did You Know?

The AJC Metropolitan Handicap (2600m), conducted during Sydney's Spring Carnival, has been a poor guide to Melbourne Cup winners in recent years. Only five horses have completed the double, starting with 'Sydney' Tim Whiffler in 1867 (to distinguish him from 'Melbourne' Tim Whiffler), and four horses back in the 1950s. Kensei finished second in 'the Metrop' before winning the Cup in 1987, but no horse has won the double in almost six decades.

Macdougal
(1959)

In 1959, the New Zealand bred gelding Macdougal (Marco Polo – Lady Fox) won a unique treble – the Brisbane Cup, the Metropolitan and the Melbourne Cup. No other horse in the history of racing has charted such an unusual pathway to Cup success, but punters shouldn't have been that surprised, Macdougal was bred at New Zealand's Trelawney Stud, the home of Foxbridge, the broodmare sire of Cup winners Hiraji (1947) and Foxzami (1949), and Alcimedes, the sire of Galilee (1966) and Silver Knight (1971).

Macdougal was a 'poddy yearling', hand-reared by Trelawney Stud groom Mary Macdougal, after whom it was named. The colt did his early racing in North Queensland before being transferred to Dick Roden in his four-year-old season. Having failed to settle in Melbourne the previous year, Macdougal came into Cup calculations with a solid second in the Hotham Handicap and went to the post in the 1959 Melbourne Cup a three length winner at 8/1.

Leading jockey Ron Hutchinson rode Macdougal in the Hotham Handicap but had a prior engagement for the Mackinnon Stakes winner Trellios. Trainer Roden secured Adelaide jockey Pat Glennon for Macdougal, and Glennon duly won his second Cup (after Comic Court in 1950) while Hutchinson, who never a rode a Cup winner, was left to lament Trellios' disappointing sixth in the race.

Record Spot

Winning Saddle Cloth Numbers

1	10	(Makybe Diva 2005)	16	2	(Piping Lane 1972)
2	7	(Delta Blues 2006)	16a	1	(Hi Jinx 1960)
3	5	(Dunaden 2011)	17	5	(Rogan Josh 1999)
4	11	(At Talaq 1986)	18	2	(Peter Pan 1932)
5	8	(Protectionist 2014)	19	7	(Prince of Penzance 2015)
6	8	(Fiorente 2013)	20	2	(Gaulus 1897)
7	2	(Just a Dash 1981)	21	2	(Shocking 2009)
8	8	(Americain 2010)	22	4	(Jezabeel 1998)
9	5	(Straight Draw 1957)	23	2	(King Ingoda 1922)
10	4	(Viewed 2008)	24	4	(Brew 2000)
11	7	(Empire Rose 1988)	25	2	(Rimfire 1948)
12	11	(Makybe Diva 2003)	26	1	(Auraria 1895)
13	6	(Ethereal 2001)	28	1	(Sasanof 1916)
14	5	(Green Moon 2012)	39	1	(Zulu 1881)
15	5	(Let's Elope 1991)			

History Spot

Hi Jinx
(1960)

The 100th running of the Melbourne Cup drew a field of 32 runners for what was billed as the 'Centenary Melbourne Cup'. Most of Australia was hoping the champion Tulloch, having recovered from a life-threatening illness that robbed him of his entire four-year-old season, could win the Cup with the weight of 10st 1lb (64kg). Alas, the 3/1 favourite got too far back in the race and ran seventh under the hard riding of Neville Selwood.

The 1960 Melbourne Cup was won by the five-year-old New Zealand mare Hi Jinx, carrying just 7st 10lb (49kg), in a close finish from fellow Kiwis Howsie and Illumquh. Tulloch proved that he was not a spent force by winning the CB Fisher Plate at WFA on the following Saturday, before finishing his stellar career with a victory in the Brisbane Cup the following June.

Did You Know?

There were 32 runners in the Centenary Melbourne Cup in 1960. The oncourse totalisator had a maximum 24 numbers, so the bottom 22 horses were bracketed in pairs (e.g. 14 and 14a down to 24a and 24b) to accommodate the extra horses. The winner Hi Jinx started at 50/1 and the mare's official number was 16a (bracketed with Essayist, No.16). Hi Jinx paid 59/6 and 15/6 a place for a £1 unit, which the backers of Essayist were also able to collect.

The Totalisator Agency Board (TAB) for off-course punters was introduced the following year, in 1961.

Even Stevens
(1962)

New Zealander Even Stevens joined a select group when the five-year-old stallion captured the Caulfield–Melbourne Cups double in 1962 under regular rider Les Coles. Having beaten the handicapper in both races, Even Stevens (by Fairs Fair) was sensationally backed to win both Cups after setting a race record in his Australian debut. The Caulfield Cup was won in a canter after Evens Stevens was allowed to bowl along in front, and not even a rehandicap in the Melbourne Cup (to 8st 5lb or 53kg) dimmed the view that the Cup was at the Kiwi's mercy.

Trainer A.McGregor took the unusual step of starting Evens Stevens in the Werribee Cup, which he won just as easily carrying 9st 5lb (59.5kg). This saw him start a prohibitive 3/1 favourite in the Cup. Even Stevens won by four lengths, from Comic Court's daughter Comicquita, with Aquinita another three lengths away in third place.

Did You Know?

The 'Fashions on the Field' was first held at the Melbourne Spring Carnival in 1961 in an attempt to attract younger people to the races. In 1965, English model Jean Shrimpton caused a sensation on Derby Day when she chose to attend the races sans gloves, stockings and hat, and with a skirt 10cm above the knee. She attended Melbourne Cup Day with a much more demure ensemble.

Record Spot

Most Successful Trainers

12 wins	Bart Cummings:	
	Light Fingers (1965) *	Galilee (1966) *
	Red Handed (1967)	Think Big (1974) *
	Think Big (1975) *	Gold and Black (1977)
	Hyperno (1979)	Kingston Rule (1990)
	Let's Elope (1991) *	Saintly (1996)
	Rogan Josh (1999)	Viewed (2008)

* trained the quinella (first and second)

Did You Know?

Bart Cummings (1927-2015) was known as 'The Cups King', having won 12 Melbourne Cups over almost six decades of racing endeavour. By the end of the 1970s, Cummings had already eclipsed Etienne de Mestre's record five Cup wins, but the Adelaide-born trainer did not train a Cup winner during the 1980s.

Having extricated himself from financial difficulties in the late 1980s, Cummings returned to train four more Cup winners and rounded off an even dozen when Viewed won in 2008 at 40/1. Bad luck, and bad weather, probably robbed Cummings of two more Cup wins (Gold in Black in 1976 and So You Think in 2010) while race favourite Big Philou was sensationally nobbled on the day of the 1969 Melbourne Cup.

But Bart never bemoaned about the bad luck he experienced in a race that was so kind to him. His record will never be bettered.

Light Fingers
(1965)

Light Fingers was hailed 'the greatest mare since Wakeful' when the gallant five-year-old overcame injury to defeat stablemate Ziema in the 1965 Melbourne Cup. In carrying a record 8st 4lb (52.5kg) for a mare, Light Fingers provided the then 37-year-old trainer Bart Cummings with the first of a record 12 Cup victories. Champion jockey Roy Higgins regarded Light Fingers as the favourite horse of his long career and affectionately named her 'mother'.

Light Fingers was originally called Close Embrace in New Zealand, but the filly's new owner was keen to rename her in line with her Le Filou older brother The Dip ('le filou' is French for 'the thief'). An AJC and VRC Oaks winner, on her way to the 1965 Melbourne Cup the diminutive Light Fingers was scratched from the Caulfield Cup but a muscle injury and a Cup start for the one-time favourite appeared unlikely.

Drifting to 15/1 in betting, Light Fingers took her place in the field and wore down her stablemate Ziema with Roy Higgins lifting the mare over the line to win by a nose. Bart Cummings joined Bill Forrester (Gaulus and The Grafter, 1897) and James Scobie (Clean Sweep and Malster, 1900) to train the Cup quinella, but he would soon better that record too.

Galilee
(1966)

Bart Cummings always regarded Galilee as the best of his Cup winners, and the manner in which the New Zealand gelding won the 1966 Melbourne Cup certainly confirms his opinion. Just as the gallant mare Light Fingers was being hailed the winner, Galilee, ridden by Johnny Miller, swept past to win by two lengths. Light Fingers stuck on under the mare's record weight (9st 1lb or 57.5kg) to claim second place and give Bart Cummings his second straight Cup quinella.

Fittingly, Galilee raced in the same ownership as Ziema, which had run second to Light Fingers the previous year. The Alcimedes four-year-old won the Toorak Handicap (1600m) and Caulfield Cup double, and primed up for the Melbourne Cup with a good third in the Mackinnon Stakes. Galilee finished Carnival week with victory in the CB Fisher Plate (2000m).

The following year, Galilee proved his staying prowess win four straight wins, culminating with an easy 6 length win in the 1967 Sydney Cup carrying 9st 10lb (60.5kg). Injury sidelined the gelding during its five-year-old season, but when Galilee returned to racing in August 1968 the signs were encouraging. Unfortunately, Galilee was unplaced in Rain Lover's Cup, having shouldered 10st 1lb (64kg) on older legs.

History Spot

Red Handed
(1967)

R ed Handed, another of the wonderfully named Le Filou progeny (The Dip, Light Fingers), provided trainer Bart Cummings with a hat trick of Melbourne Cup victories. Ridden by jockey Roy Higgins, Red Handed proved too strong for Red Crest in the run to the line and won by neck, with Floodbird a neck away in third place.

Red Handed showed early promise in a stable full of stars, and was able to match it with Ziema and Galilee on the training track. A fall in the 1966 Geelong Cup put any plans for a Melbourne Cup campaign on hold for another year, but in the Spring of 1967 Red Handed ran seconds to Tobin Bronze in the Toorak Handicap and Caulfield Cup and came right into calculations.

Red Handed's fourth in the Mackinnon Stakes, Cummings' traditional Melbourne Cup lead up, saw the Le Filou gelding go out as the 4/1 equal favourite. Red Handed saluted the judge after Higgins outrode rival Ron Taylor in a punishing finish. It was Higgins' second and last Melbourne Cup win, but Bart Cummings was only getting started.

Record Spot

Record Time	
3.19.1	Rain Lover (1968) empirical (2 miles)
3.16.3	Kingston Rule (1990) metric (3200m)

Did You Know?

Rain Lover established several records in winning the 1968 Melbourne Cup. Rain Lover won by eight lengths, equalling the winning margin set by Archer in the inaugural Cup, and ran a record time of 3:19.1. When Australia adopted the metric system in 1972, the distance of the race was reduced by 18.7 metres (61.3ft) and Rain Lover's 1968 race record of 3:19.1 was adjusted to 3:17.9 as the new benchmark.

Rain Lover came back twelve months later and won a second successive Cup – only the second horse to do so after Archer (Peter Pan won in 1932 and 1934) – to join a select group of dual Melbourne Cup winners.

History Spot

Rain Lover
(1968–69)

Rain Lover (Latin Lover GB – Rain Spot) was bred by Clifford Reid, who also bred the 1945 Melbourne Cup winner Rainbird. Previously trained by Grahame Heagney, Rain Lover was transferred to Heagney's foreman Mick Robbins when the Adelaide trainer went to the US to train his star Tobin Bronze. Robbins was a former miner who had only taken up his trainer's license three months before Rain Lover came into his Adelaide stable.

The four-year-old was ridden by Jim Johnson, who had piloted Gatum Gatum (which had raced in similar colours and ownership) to Cup success in 1963. Rain Lover disappointed in the Caulfield Cup, but bounced back to form with a win in the Mackinnon Stakes. Carrying 8st 2lb (51.5kg) in the Melbourne Cup, Rain Lover was a weighted certainly after winning at WFA the previous Saturday and started at 7/1, behind race favourites Lowland and Artic Coast at 6/1. Rain Lover won the Cup by a record equalling margin of eight lengths in race record time.

A year later, Rain Lover shouldered 9st 7lb (60.5kg) to outstay the well-backed lightweight Alsop (7st 7lb or 47.5kg) to win the Cup by a head. There was a sensation before the race when pre-post favourite Big Philou, trained by Bart Cummings, was scratched. It was later discovered that Big Philou had been 'nobbled' by a stable hand on the orders of SP bookies. The following year, Big Philou defeated Rain Lover in a match race, but one can only speculate what would have happened if they had both contested the 1969 Melbourne Cup.

Record Spot

Colour of Melbourne Cup Winners

Bay	66	(Prince of Penzance 2015)
Brown	38	(Rogan Josh 1999)
Chestnut	34	(Media Puzzle 2002)
Grey	6	(Efficient 2007)
Bay/Brown	6	(Americain 2010)
Black	3	(Clean Sweep 1900)
Black/brown	2	(White Nose 1931)

Did You Know?

Grey horses do not have a great record in the Melbourne Cup. In 155 runnings of the Cup, only 6 greys have saluted the judge (3.9%). The first grey to win the Cup was Toryboy in 1865, and it wasn't until 82 years later that another grey was first past the post when Hiraji was successful in 1947. Two decades later, greys won back to back Cups with Bagdad Note (1970) and Silver Knight (1971) saluting the judge. The next grey to win the Cup was Subzero (1992), a popular winner which later became a clerk of the course's mount at Flemington. The sixth and last grey was VRC Derby winner Efficient (2007) which, although sound, was certainly good enough to win several Cups according to owner Lloyd Williams.

History Spot

Silver Knight
(1971)

New Zealand grey Silver Knight defeated a host of Australian favourites to secure the 1971 Melbourne Cup. By Alcimedes out of Cuban Fox (by Foxbridge), Silver Knight was bred by Seton Otway at Cambridge's Trelawney Stud, the home of Cup winners Hiraji (1947), Foxzami (1949), Macdougal (1959), Hi Jinx (1960) and Polo Prince (1964).

Silver Knight ran second in the Mackinnon Stakes leading up to its Cup win, in which it started at 10/1. Igloo, one of the unluckiest horses in racing history, ran second (as it had done in the Cox Plate and Caulfield Cup), with Queenslander Tails (a son of Dalray) third. Among the beaten brigade were Big Philou, attempting a comeback after being nobbled before the 1969 Melbourne Cup, and the Caulfield Cup winner Gay Icarus, which started a short-priced 7/4 favourite.

Did You Know?

Silver Knight became only the fifth, and the last, Cup winner to sire a subsequent Cup winner when Black Knight won the race in 1984. Grand Flaneur (1880) sired Bravo (1889) and Patron (1894); Malua sired Malvolio (1891); Comedy King (1910) sired Artilleryman (1919) and King Ingoda (1922); and Spearfelt (1926) sired Dark Felt (1943).

Peter Pan (1932 and 1934) went close when his progeny Peter finished second to Sirius in 1944. Carbine's champion son, the Sydney Cup winner Wallace, sired Cup winners Kingsburgh (1914) and Patrobas (1915). Trenton, twice-placed in the Melbourne Cup (1885-86) sired the Cup winners Auraria (1895) and Revenue (1901).

History Spot

Piping Lane
(1972)

Piping Lane was an unfashionable Tasmanian stayer prepared by George Hanlon, who had learned his trade as a trainer of stayers from Jim Cummings, the father of Bart Cummings, in Adelaide. Piping Lane carried 48kg to victory in the 1972 Melbourne Cup at 40/1, beating the better performed 7/2 favourite Magnifique (53.5kg) and popular favourite Gunsynd (60.5kg) into third place.

Adelaide jockey John Letts had never ridden at Flemington before and had never set eyes on his Cup mount. Letts tasted Cups success again on Beldale Ball (1980) while George Hanlon won another two Cups, with Arwon (1978) and Black Night (1984).

Did You Know?

The 1972 Melbourne Cup was the first 'metric' Cup conducted after Australia changed from empirical measures to the metric system in 1972. The race distance of two miles (3.219 km) was shortened to 3,200 metres (1.988 mi), cutting a distance of 61.3 feet (18.7 metres) from the race.

If the race was still run over the traditional two miles, that extra 18 or so metres would have changed many results over the past 40 years!

Opposite: Piper Lane, ridden by Johnny Letts, defeats Magnifique (inside) Gunsynd (grey, centre), Double Irish (centre obscured and Stormy Seas (outside) in the 1972 Melbourne Cup.

Record Spot

Most Successful Jockeys

4 wins	Harry White: *
	Think Big (1974)
	Think Big (1975)
	Arwon (1978)
	Hyperno (1979)

* tied with Bobby Lewis

Did You Know?

Harry White (b.1944) won his four Melbourne Cups during the 1970s – as opposed to the 25 years it took co-record holder Bobby Lewis to set the same record. Although he rode until 1995, White could not improve on his Cup record to make it his own. Three of White's winners were for master trainer Bart Cummings, with whom he had a long association, while Arwon was trained by George Hanlon.

White rode in 24 Melbourne Cups, and won 200 feature races including 60 Group 1's during his career. In 2015, the VRC announced that Melbourne Cup-winning jockeys would be honoured with the presentation of a gold whip named after Harry White.

History Spot

Think Big
(1974–75)

Bart Cummings' bonny mare Leilani was all the rage in 1974. The AJC Oaks winner won the Toorak Handicap (1600m), Turnbull Stakes (2000m), Caulfield Cup (2400m) and Mackinnon Stakes (2000m) that Spring and was a firm 7/2 favourite for the Melbourne Cup. The only question mark concerned the slightly-framed Leilani's ability to carry a record 55.5kg over two miles.

Meanwhile, the form of Cummings' other Cup hope, the similarly New Zealand-bred Think Big, was coming into focus. The four-year-old son of Sobig had run third to Igloo in the 1974 Brisbane Cup the previous season but had finished last in Leilani's Caulfield Cup. Think Big's win in the Hotham Handicap on Derby Day brought the gelding back into calculations as a 12/1 chance in the Cup, but few could have anticipated the manner in which it flew past Leilani inside the final 100m to win by a length. Cummings had trained the Cup quinella again, but had the best horse won the race?

Think Big did not win another race in the next twelve months, but was given top weight of 58.5kg in the 1975 Melbourne Cup. On a rain-soaked track, Think Big started at 33/1 but powered through the mud to defeat stablemate Holiday Wagon by a long neck. Cummings had done it again, as well as training another Cups quinella, and Think Big could not be denied his place among the great Melbourne Cup winners.

Van Der Hum
(1976)

The 1976 Melbourne Cup was almost called off after a torrential downpour turned Flemington racecourse in to a lake prior to the start of the race. A deluge opened up just before the official starting time of 2.10pm, and the race was delayed 40 minutes before the field was sent on their way. As the runners entered the straight, covered head to toe in mud with jockey colours and saddlecloth numbers indistinguishable, a dark form surged to the front in the final 200m. The name? Van der Hum ... roughly translated, 'what's his name' ridden by Bob Skelton.

Van der Hum was ready-made for Cup success on a bog track. New Zealand-bred, the son of Hermes (GB) had been schooled as a hurdler by trainer Len Robinson before being brought to Australia. Van der Hum ran a good third to How's Now in the Caulfield Cup, so it was no outsider in Cup betting, and the rain on Cup day saw the five-year-old backed into 9/2 favouritism. Bart Cummings' Gold and Black ran a good second, but received 10lb (4.5kg) in weight from the winner and would get his chance on a firmer track twelve months later. Reckless, which ran fourth in the race, would also play his part in a dramatic 1977 Melbourne Cup.

History Spot
Gold and Black
(1977)

Gold and Black avenged an unlucky second in the 1976 Cup with an authoritative length win over Reckless in the 1977 Melbourne Cup. The Tommy Woodcock-trained Reckless carried immense sentimental support around the country, but the race proved a triumph for Bart Cummings and earned the trainer the outright record with six Cup wins.

Tommy Woodcock, then 71 years old, had been the strapper for the immortal Phar Lap and had been by the gelding's side when the champion died in the US in April 1932. The previous Autumn, Reckless had won the Sydney Cup (defeating Gold and Black), Adelaide Cup and Brisbane Cup in quick succession. Gold and Black, however, had the Bart Cummings polish and the services of jockey John Duggan in the 1977 Cup.

Gold and Black started 7/2 favourite on the strength of the five-year-old gelding's win in the Mackinnon Stakes, with Reckless firm at 11/2. As Gold and Black surged to the front at the 200m, Reckless challenged on his inside but faded in the run to the line. Some thought Woodcock had gone too light on Reckless and should have given him a hit out on the Saturday. Reckless later broke down in running third in the Perth Cup and was retired.

The Geoff Murphy trained Hyperno ran third in the 1977 Melbourne Cup and would also return to claim his place in the Cup's history – but only after a change of trainers.

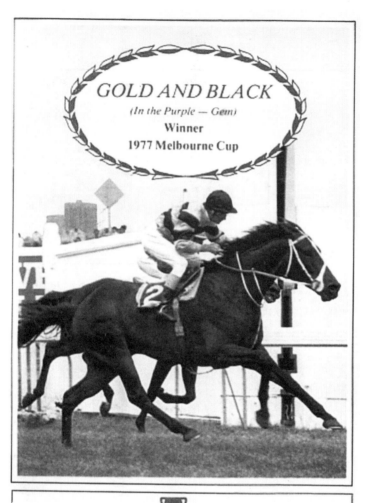

GOLD AND BLACK
(In the Purple — Gem)
Winner
1977 Melbourne Cup

Victoria Racing Club | *Melbourne Cup Carnival*

The Melbourne Cup

Flemington, Tuesday, November 7, 1978

OFFICIAL PROGRAMME   PRICE 30 CENTS

History Spot

Arwon
(1978)

New Zealand-bred Arwon was originally named Flash Guy, but after being brought by a group of owners from Nowra on NSW's south coast (the birthplace of the great Archer), the gelding was renamed Arwon, which is Nowra backwards.

Arwon was a talented, but difficult, horse to train before finding a home with Melbourne Cup-winning trainer George Hanlon. In the Spring of 1978, Arwon ran a close second to the Bart Cummings-trained Ming Dynasty in the AJC Metropolitan before losing a controversial photo-finished to the Tommy Smith-trained Taksan in the Caulfield Cup. Arwon looked to have won the race, but his second placing may have been a blessing in disguise. Arwon did not receive a penalty for the Melbourne Cup, in which it carried just 50.5kg.

Ridden by Harry White, Arwon surged to the lead at the 200m mark and held off late challenges from Dandaleith and Karu to win by a half-neck. Cox Plate winner So Called started favourite at 11/2 but failed to run out a strong two miles. After its retirement, Arwon became a mounted police horse.

Opposite: The official race book for the 1978 Melbourne Cup, which was won by Arwon. The cover featured the previous year's winner Gold and Black. When the VRC puts the Cup winner on the cover of their racebooks on the actual year they run, they'll sell like hot cakes!

History Spot

Hyperno
(1979)

Given the choice between riding Hyperno and Salamander in the 1979 Melbourne Cup, 'The Professor' Roy Higgins chose Salamander. Having previously ridden Hyperno in the 1978 Mooney Valley Cup (which was run in the Autumn), Higgins failed to ride his mount out to the line and the temperamental gelding was beaten on the post by Sydney stayer Clear Day. Higgins was suspended for the ride which later influenced his decision not to ride Hyperno in the 1979 Cup – to his everlasting regret.

After a third placing in the 1977 Melbourne Cup, Hyperno won the Adelaide Cup in 1978 before going amiss and being transferred to Bart Cummings' stable. Carrying 56kg in the 1979 Melbourne Cup and ridden by Harry White, Hyperno beat Salamander by a nose after a titanic battle over the last 200m. The tragedy of the race was the death of 3/1 favourite Dulcify, which had to be put down after being galloped on from behind (by Hyperno, ironically).

Hyperno started favourite in the 1980 Melbourne Cup and finished an unlucky seventh to Beldale Ball after being boxed in on the fence for most of the straight. The following year, the eight-year-old competed in his fourth Cup, running a creditable sixth behind Just a Dash.

Beldale Ball
(1980)

Racing can be a cruel and sometimes luckless sport. Twelve months after the champion Dulcify was destroyed after breaking its pelvis in the 1979 Melbourne Cup, South Australian trainer Colin Hayes broke through for his first win in the Melbourne Cup with the American import Beldale Ball. In reality, Dulcify would have carried Beldale Ball on his back and won the Melbourne Cup, but Hayes took the win with good grace. The Cup was that hard race to win!

Beldale Ball was owned by English owner Robert Sangster, and ridden by popular jockey Johnny Letts who rated the lightweight (49.5kg) well in front and led all the way to win. Beldale Ball put the writing on the wall with victory in the Hotham Handicap (then called the Dalgety Handicap) on Derby Day.

The scratching or pre-post favourite Kingston Town threw markets into turmoil prior to the race, and Beldale Ball started at the good odds of 11/1 as punters backed previous Cup winners Hyperno (3/1 favourite) and Arwon (10/1).

History Spot

Gurner's Lane
(1982)

Trainer Tommy Smith and millionaire owner David Hains watched from the Flemington grandstand as Kingston Town ran to the lead in the 1982 Melbourne Cup, but they failed to see the horse darting through on the champion gelding's inside in the final 100m of the race. When the cheer went up, they were sure Kingston Town had won the Cup. By the time they had gotten to the bottom of the stairs, the winning number had gone up in the official judge's frame. It was No.4. Gurner's Lane.

Sir Tristram gelding Gurner's Lane was owned by a syndicate of 39 owners headed by Andrew Ramsden, later the Chairman of the VRC. The chestnut ran third in the AJC Metropolitan before winning the Caulfield Cup, after which it incurred a 3kg penalty for the Melbourne Cup. Trainer Geoff Murphy complained that Kingston Town was 'thrown in' at the weights at just 59kg, especially after the champion won its third straight Cox Plate, and that his gelding was too closely weighted to him to win.

The handicapper was proved right with Gurner's Lane winning by a neck. Punters didn't know what to make of the form, and sent Smith's other galloper Just a Dash out as 11/2 favourite. In the aftermath of the race, Kingston Town's rider Malcolm Johnston was heavily criticised for taking 'The King' to lead far too early at the top of the straight. Gurner's Lane's jockey Mick Dittman rode a masterly race, but was later suspended for poleaxing Port Carling (also trained by Tommy Smith) as he sped through a gap on the fence.

Kingston Town later broke down during his Perth campaign that Summer while Gurner's Lane did not win another race.

Record Spot

Best Horses NOT to win a Melbourne Cup

Malster (1900)	Leilani (1974)
Wakeful (1903)	Reckless (1977)
Eurythmic (1921)	Kingston Town (1982)
Manfred (1925)	Super Impose (1988)
Beau Vite (1941)	Veandercross (1992)
Redcraze (1956)	Tie the Knot (1998)
Tulloch (1960)	Vinnie Roe (2004)
Big Philou (1969)	So You Think (2010)
Gunsynd (1971)	

Did You Know?

When Kingston Town was beaten on the line by Gurner's Lane in the 1982 Melbourne Cup, the hearts of all true racing fans – even those who didn't back him – were broken. The Cup would have been 'The King's' crowning glory in a career that saw him capture three Cox Plates, the AJC and Queensland Derbies and a Sydney Cup among his 30 career wins. Arguably the best horse to emerge since Phar Lap (even better than Tulloch?), Kingston Town joined a pantheon of racing greats which tried – and through bad luck, bad timing or bad management – failed to win the Melbourne Cup.

1/11/83 VRC R5   1/11/83 VR

History Spot

Kiwi
(1983)

The New Zealand gelding Kiwi, ridden by twenty-year-old jockey Jim Cassidy, unleashed a withering burst in the straight to win the 1983 Melbourne Cup by one and three quarters lengths from Noble Comment and Mr Jazz. Kiwi was in a seemingly impossible position at the 400m mark and only hit the front at the 50m, but won the race going away from the rest of the field. It was an amazing performance from an unfashionably bred gelding ... perhaps even the best Cup win of them all.

Kiwi was bought by trainer 'Snow' Lupton and his wife for $1,000 as a stock horse to round up sheep on their property. The son of Blarney Kiss showed enough dash around the paddocks to convince his owners that he had a career as a racehorse. The Luptons were patient with the gelding, but after winning their hometown Wellington Cup with the five-year-old, they set their sights on the 1983 Melbourne Cup.

Kiwi won the Cup at his first Australian start in spectacular fashion, but his reputation preceded him and the six-year-old started at the safe odds of 9/1 and a New Zealand folk hero was born. Kiwi was scratched from the 1984 Cup, was unplaced in 1985 and ran a great fourth to At Talaq in 1986 – as a nine-year-old – despite pulling up lame.

Opposite: The official photo finish of Kiwi's Cup triumph in 1983. No other horse is in sight ...

Record Spot

Melbourne Cup prize money over the years

1861	£930	1863	£510
1865	£1034	1882	£2010
1887	£4005	1889	£7237
1890	£13,230	1898	£3,524
1921	£10,450	1930	£12,429
1944	£7,700	1952	£14,550
1960	£25,750	1966	$62,000
1971	$102,000	1978	$210,000
1983	$310,000	1984	$535,000
1985	$1,024,000	1990	$2,035,000
2000	$3,035,000	2001	$4,075,000
2005	$5,100,000	2015	$6,200,000

Did You Know?

The first million-dollar Melbourne Cup, with $650,000 going to the winner, was run in 1985. Won by the hardy gelding What a Nuisance, the 1985 Cup was also the first to be sponsored and was officially known as The Fosters' Melbourne Cup. The winning trophies were presented to high profile owner Lloyd Williams by Prince Charles and his then wife Princess Diana.

Today, the Melbourne Cup is worth $6.2 million dollars, which makes it the second highest valued stakes race behind the Dubai World Cup ($10 million). Emirates, the world's largest Middle Eastern airline, has been the sponsor of the Melbourne Cup since 1997.

History Spot

At Talaq
(1986)

At Talaq was bought by Sheikh Hamdan bin Rashid Al Maktoum for $800,000 at the Fasig Tipton Saratoga Yearling Sale and sent to England to be trained by Harry Thomson Jones. The son of Roberto (USA) raced successfully in Europe, winning the Grand Prix de Paris at Longchamp, before being sent to Colin Hayes in Australia.

With the Melbourne Cup boasting $1,000,000 in prize money, wealthy overseas owners began to eye off Australia's greatest race. At Talaq joined the Colin Hayes stable in his six-year-old season, winning the Mackinnon Stakes before his determined victory in the 1986 Melbourne Cup. In both races, At Talaq was ridden by Hayes' stable rider Michael Clarke. The Entire started at 10/1 in the Cup because of concerns he might be 'too brilliant' to win a two mile race. How wrong they were!

At Talaq held on to win by a long neck from Rising Fear, which was prepared by hobby trainer and noted cartoonist Larry Pickering, with New Zealander Sea Legend a neck away third. Former Melbourne Cup winner Kiwi (1983) was fourth, future Melbourne Cup winner Empire Rose (1988) was fifth and the previous year's Cup winner Black Knight finished down the track.

RS   1/11/88 V.R.C.   V.R.C.

Empire Rose
(1988)

It was a case of third time lucky for New Zealand's Empire Rose when the mare won the 1988 Melbourne Cup. Empire Rose had run fifth in 1986, and second to Kensei in 1987, but put the writing on the wall that she was ready to go one better when she swept down the outside and won the 1988 Mackinnon Stakes on Derby Day.

Following her second placing to Kensei in the 1987 Melbourne Cup, Empire Rose returned home and won the New Zealand Cup over 3200m. The mare's owners, the Brodie family who also bred her and her dam Summer Fleur, considered retiring the daughter of the all-conquering Sir Tristram to stud, but decided to give her one more go at winning the Melbourne Cup.

Empire Rose started at 5/1 equal favouite with the Metropolitan winner Natski (Mick Dittman), and held on to beat that horse by half a head in 1988's 'Bicentenary' Melbourne Cup. Natski looked sure to win in the final 100m of the race but Empire Rose, ridden by Tony Allan, was such a big mare, and with such a big heart, that Natski just couldn't get past her.

Opposite: The official photo finish of the 1988 Melbourne Cup shows just how big the mare Empire Rose was and how close Natski got to her.

Record Spot

Most Successful Trainers

5 wins	Lee Freedman:
	Tawriffic (1989) *
	Subzero (1992)
	Doriemus (1995)
	Makybe Diva (2004)
	Makybe Diva (2005)

* also trained first and second

Did You Know?

In the 1980s, NSW-born Lee Freedman (born 1965) headed up a training team known as 'FBI' – Freedman Brothers Incorporated – involving his brothers Richard, Anthony, Michael and Mark. The Freedmans are the great grandsons of three-time Melbourne Cup winning jockey Bill 'Midge' MacLachlan (Prince Foote 1909, Comedy King 1910 and Westcourt 1917).

The Freedman brothers relocated from Warwick Farm after being unable to secure stables at Randwick and settled at Flemington in 1984. Five years later, Freedman trained first and second in the Melbourne Cup – Tawriffic and Super Impose – and followed up with further wins with Subzero (1992) and Doriemus (1995).

After Makybe Diva's first Melbourne Cup success in 2003, Freedman took over the training of the mare when trainer David Hall relocated to Hong Kong. Freedman then won two more Melbourne Cups with the champion mare before announcing his retirement from training in 2011 after a period of ill-health.

Kingston Rule
(1990)

Kingston Rule may well be the best bred Melbourne Cup winner of the modern era. The chestnut gelding was bred by David Hains, the owner of Kingston Town, who mated his champion mare Rose of Kingston with the champion American stallion Secretariat. Rose of Kingston won the AJC Derby–VRC Oaks double in 1982 and was named Australian Racehorse of the Year, while Secretariat had captured the three-year-old 'Triple Crown' in the USA. The ensuing foal was named Kingston Rule.

For a horse bred to be racing royalty, Kingston Rule looked unlikely to rise to any great heights on his arrival in Australia. When the Entire ran 35 lengths last on a heavy track in his first Australian start for Tommy Smith (the trainer of Kingston Town), Smith recommended that the horse be gelded. Hains however wanted to maintain Kingston Rule as a stud proposition and transferred the four-year-old to Bart Cummings.

Cummings found the secret to Kingston Rule – the horse liked firm going – and trained him as an out and out stayer. By-passing the Caulfield Cup, Kingston Rule won the Mooney Valley Cup and ran second in the Dalgety (Hotham Handicap) leading into the 1990 Melbourne Cup. Superbly ridden by Darren Beadman, Kingston Rule defeated 7/1 equal favourite The Phantom and set a race record of 3:16.3, which still stands.

Although Kingston Rule's stud career wasn't a great success, the 1990 Melbourne Cup win confirmed David Hains' opinion of the horse and was some small compensation for his champion Kingston Town's unlucky second in 1982.

Let's Elope
(1991)

New Zealand-bred mare Let's Elope came from obscurity in the Spring of 1991 to win the Turnbull Stakes, Caulfield Cup, Mackinnon Stakes and Melbourne Cup in quick succession. In flying under the radar before entering the Bart Cummings stable, the Nassipour mare carried just 51kg in the Melbourne Cup – after incurring a 3kg penalty after a thrilling Caulfield Cup victory – to beat stablemate Shiva's Revenge in a controversial finish.

Let's Elope's record as a three-year-old in New Zealand was encouraging enough for owners Dennis Marks and Kevin White to purchase her for $150,000 and give her to Cummings to train. Let's Elope proved wayward in her races, and jockey Steven King had to survive a protest from runner-up Shiva's Revenge (Shane Dye) to complete the Cups double. The following year, Let's Elope won three straight races culminating in a record-breaking win in the Australian Cup, again defeating the ill-fated Shiva's Revenge.

Let's Elope finished second in the 1992 Cox Plate, but was relegated to fifth for causing inference. After suffering a bleeding attack, the same fate befell her in a Group 1 race in the US before injury forced the mare into retirement.

Record Spot

Adelaide Cup – Melbourne Cup	
1884	Malua
1968	Rain Lover
1981	Just a Dash
1992	Subzero

Did You Know?

In the 1970s and 1980s at least, the Adelaide Cup (2 miles/3200m) was deemed a good guide for Melbourne Cup success at year's end, especially for late blooming three-year-olds entering their four-year-old season. Rain Lover (1968) was the first three-year-old to capture the Adelaide Cup–Melbourne Cup double in a calendar year. In 1981, Sydney trainer Tommy Smith sent three-year-old gelding Just a Dash to Adelaide to claim the SAJC St. Leger-Adelaide Cup double. Just over a decade later, trainer Lee Freedman's grey gelding Subzero took the South Australia Derby-Adelaide Cup double. Both horses duly won the Melbourne Cup in their respective four-year-old seasons.

Malua won the Cups double back in 1884 as an older horse, while two others achieved the double in a non-calendar year. King Ingoda followed its 1922 Melbourne Cup win with success in the following year's Adelaide Cup (1923). After running third to Gold and Black in the 1977, Hyperno captured the 1978 Adelaide Cup for trainer Geoff Murphy. A year later, after transferring to the Bart Cummings stable, Hyperno won the Melbourne Cup.

In 2006, however, Adelaide changed its public holiday from May to March, pushing the Adelaide Cup to much earlier in the Autumn. The race was downgraded to a Group 2 race and no longer serves as a guide to Melbourne Cup success.

Vintage Crop
(1993)

Vintage Crop's victory in the 1993 Melbourne Cup put the great race on the international map and opened the floodgates as far as northern hemisphere-trained horses were concerned. The six-year-old chestnut gelding won the Curragh Cup and the Irish St Leger after spending a brief career contesting hurdles. Trainer Dermot Weld set Vintage Crop for the Melbourne Cup in September 1993 and the gelding set the mould for international horses by winning the Cup first up.

The Flemington track was soaked before the 1993 Melbourne Cup by overnight rain, which certainly played to the visitors' strong suit. Ridden by Irish jockey Mick Kinane with 55.5kg, Vintage Crop started at 14/1 and ploughed through the mud to win the Cup by three lengths from roughies Te Akau Nick (160/1) and Mercator (125/1).

Vintage Crop won the Irish St Leger for a second time before returning to Australia and competing in the 1994 and 1995 Melbourne Cups, finishing seventh and third respectively. The son of Rousillon (USA) out of the Irish mare Overplay is honoured with a statue on the Curragh Racecourse.

History Spot

Jeune
(1994)

Jeune began his racing career in Europe with some success before Melbourne Cup-winning owner Sheikh Hamdan bin Rashid Al Maktoum (At Talaq 1986) sent the Entire to Australia at the end of his four-year-old season to be trained by David Hayes. By Kalaglow from the Green Dancer mare Youthful, Jeune was bred for stamina but the stallion's lack of staying credentials left a huge question mark over its ability to run a strong two miles.

In Australia, Jeune won the Underwood Stakes (1800m) and ran good seconds in the Caulfield Stakes (2000m) and Mackinnon Stakes (2000m) either side on an unplaced run in the Cox Plate after being knocked out of the race. Jeune carried a good horse's weight of 56.5kg in the Melbourne Cup and starting at 16/1, defeated the Caulfield Cup winner Paris Lane by two lengths on a wet track.

Jeune was ridden by former champion apprentice Wayne Harris, who had to overcome serious illness to resume his riding career in the early 1990s. Harris took the ride after Shane Dye (Tawriffic 1989) knocked back the mount and also steered Jeune to wins in the 1995 Orr Stakes and Graiglee Stakes, and a close second in the BMW Stakes at Randwick, before the horse was retired to stud. Jeune sired the Caulfield Cup winner Mummify (2003) and Melbourne Cup runner-up On A Jeune (2005).

History Spot

Doriemus
(1995)

Twelve months before Doriemus won the 1995 Melbourne Cup, trainer Lee Freedman gave anyone who wanted to listen the tip that his new staying star was a champion in the making. The fact Doriemus was then a beaten favourite in the 1994 Sandown Cup, and had a light and winless Winter in Brisbane the following year, made people forget about the five-year-old gelding. The son of Norman Pentaquad (USA) and the skill of champion premier Melbourne jockey Damian Oliver changed all that.

Doriemus was winless in the Spring of 1995 but a good second in the Turnbull Stakes (2000m) saw the gelding sent out an 8/1 chance in the Caulfield Cup. Carrying 52kg, Doriemus earned a 2.5kg penalty after his neck win over Count Chivas, but trainer Lee Freedman followed the trend set by international visitors and did not start Doriemus again before the Melbourne Cup. Starting at 10/1, Doriemus defeated the VRC Derby winner Nothin' Leica Dane and 1993 Cup winner Vintage Crop on a heavy track to give Damian Oliver his first Cup, and trainer Lee Freedman his third.

Doriemus proved to be one of the most consistent stayers of the modern era, winning the 1996 AJC Queen Elizabeth Stakes (2000m) and Turnbull Stakes (2000m) before running placings in the 1997 Caulfield Cup, 1997 Melbourne Cup, 1998 Mercedes Classic, 1998 Sydney Cup and 1998 AJC Metropolitan Handicap. Doriemus was retired after being unplaced in the 1998 Melbourne Cup, his fourth attempt at the race.

History Spot

Saintly
(1996)

Saintly was a special horse for trainer Bart Cummings. The champion trainer bred the chestnut gelding, which was sired by his former star three-year-old Skychase out of the Sir Tristram mare All Grace in 1992. He even brought business partner Dato' Tan Chin Nam (Think Big) into the ownership. Saintly won the Australian Cup as a three-year-old and was placed behind the great Octagonal in the Rosehill Guineas, Mercedes Classic and the AJC Derby.

In the Spring of 1996, Saintly started odds on in the AJC Metropolitan Handicap, but could only run third. Just when punters were doubting the horse's staying ability, trainer Bart Cummings weaved his magic and won the Cox Plate–Melbourne Cup double with his chestnut at its next two starts. Patiently ridden by Darren Beadman in the Cup, Saintly surged to the lead to defeat the 1996 Sydney Cup winner Count Chivas with Skybeau third.

Saintly won the Orr Stakes (1400m) first up in 1997 but then tragically broke down and never raced again. Saintly's Melbourne Cup win was certainly a good omen for Darren Beadman. The popular jockey later announced his retirement, for a time, to become a Christian preacher. When queried about his decision by mentor Bart Cummings, Beadman told him he had been 'called by the Lord'. Cummings' response was priceless.

'Get a second opinion.'

History Spot
Might and Power
(1997)

Might and Power joined the ranks of the great front-runners of Australia horseracing when the Zabeel gelding led all the way to win the 1997 Caulfield Cup–Melbourne Cup double. Superbly ridden by Jimmy Cassidy, Might and Power won the Caulfield Cup by an imposing seven lengths, and then held on to win the Melbourne Cup by a nose. In both cases, Might and Power relegated the 1995 Caulfield Cup–Melbourne Cup winner to second place.

Might and Power was originally bought by Anthony Cummings for owner Nick Moraitis, but a falling out between trainer and owner saw the horse transferred to the media-shy Jack Denham. Might and Power showed some ability as a late three-year-old but the horse disappointed in the Sydney Spring Carnival when it was tried over sprint distances. A change in jockey and state saw Might and Power blitz the Caulfield Cup field in record time, but the gelding incurred a 3.5kg penalty for the Melbourne Cup, which saw it carry 56kg.

In the 1997 Melbourne Cup, Might and Power led all the way to hold off the fast finishing Doriemus (57.5kg) by a nose. Greg Hall, the jockey of Doriemus, flashed his whip in a victory salute after the line, but it was Jimmy Cassidy and Might and Power that prevailed in the official photo finish. Might and Power went on to win the Mercedes Classic (BMW Stakes 2400m), AJC Queen Elizabeth Stakes (2000m), Doomben Cup (2020m), Cox Plate (2040m) and VRC Elizabeth Stakes (2500m) to stamp itself as the World Champion Stayer of 1997–98.

Record Spot

Auckland Cup (NZ) – Melbourne Cup

1998   Jezabeel

Did You Know?

The New Zealand mare Jezabeel (Zabeel-Passefleur) is the only winner of the Auckland Cup–Melbourne Cup double. Run over 2 miles (3200m), the Auckland Cup was traditionally run on New Year's Day but was switched to March in 2007. Because the race is run so early in the year, it has had little bearing on the Melbourne Cup over the years, although 1992 winner Castletown later ran third to Subzero and Veandercross that year.

Trained by Brian Jenkins, Jezabeel defeated another Kiwi mare, Champagne, in a controversial 1998 Melbourne Cup. Jezabeel had been knocked out of contention in the Caulfield Cup that year, by eventual winner Taufan's Melody no less, and did not race again before the Melbourne Cup. Backed into 6/1 favouritism after a huge betting plunge sparked by the late Kerry Packer, Jezabeel made the most of the Flemington track's front-runner bias that year to fight back under the riding of jockey Chris Munce to win by a long neck.

Record Spot

Mackinnon Stakes – Melbourne Cup

1884	Malua
1890	Carbine
1930	Phar Lap
1932	Peter Pan
1934	Peter Pan
1937	The Trump
1950	Comic Court
1951	Delta
1952	Dalray
1954	Rising Fast
1968	Rain Lover
1986	At Talaq
1988	Empire Rose
1991	Let's Elope
1999	Rogan Josh

Did You Know?

The Mackinnon Stakes was originally known as the Melbourne Stakes before being renamed in honour of VRC chairman L.K.S. Mackinnon, in 1937. Run on Derby Day over 2000m under weight-for-age conditions, the Mackinnon Stakes was traditionally viewed as an ideal lead up race to the Melbourne Cup three days later.

Malua (1884) was the first horse to complete the double, with some of the turf's greatest names achieving the same feat – Phar Lap (1930), Peter Pan (1932 and 1934), Comic Court (1950), Rising Fast (1954), Rain Lover (1968) and Let's Elope (1991) to name but a few.

The main problem that plagued the race, however, was that many trainers used the Mackinnon Stakes as a 'warm up' to the Melbourne Cup (the race was cynically called 'The Warm Up' Stakes by punters for many years). Horses carrying huge weights at weight for age would be storming home at the end of the 2000m, and then carry much less over a further distance in the Cup.

The VRC tried to combat this by making the race a Group 1 and increasing the race's value to $500,000. Regardless, many trainers started to avoid the race, preferring to keep their horses fresh for Tuesday's Cup so its relevance as a Cup guide diminished in the new millennium. After Rogan Josh (1999), which actually won the race, no Melbourne Cup winner has even contested the Mackinnon Stakes.

In 2016, the VRC made the decision to switch the Mackinnon Stakes with the 1600m Emirates Stakes (held on the Saturday after the Cup), meaning the era of 'The Warm Up' Stakes was well and truly over.

History Spot

Rogan Josh
(1999)

If there was any need to prove the genius of Bart Cummings as a master trainer of stayers, you need look no further than the success of Rogan Josh in 1999. With the agreement of trainer Colin Webster, owner Wendy Green badgered Cummings to take over the training of the West Australian gelding after the lightly-raced six-year-old had run a close second in the 1998 Perth Cup. Cummings agreed because he liked the fact that the horse had not started racing until it was four years old and was Australian bred (by Old Spice out of Eastern Mystique).

Cummings entrusted Rogan Josh's Spring campaign to his former star apprentice John Marshall. Rogan Josh won the Herbert Power Handicap in October and then ran a slashing fourth in the 1999 Caulfield Cup. In a traditional Cummings Cups campaign, Rogan Josh took his place in the WFA Mackinnon Stakes on Derby Day and burst into Melbourne Cup calculations with a slashing win at 12/1.

Starting a 6/1 second favourite, Rogan Josh prevailed in a driving finish to beat the Godolphin-trained Central Park with the dead-heaters Zazabelle (also trained by Cummings) and Lahar in third place. Rogan Josh became only the third West Australian horse to win the Melbourne Cup, following the success of Blue Spec (1905) and Black Night (1984) but like many Cup winners was fated never to win another race.

History Spot

Brew
(2000)

The ingeniously named New Zealand gelding Brew (by Sir Tristram out of the Japan Cup-winning mare Horlicks) scraped into the final field of 24 runners of the 2000 Millennium Melbourne Cup with a win in the Saab Quality (Hotham Handicap) on Derby Day. Carrying just 49kg, Brew was ridden by twenty-year-old Kerrin McEvoy to a two-length win at the odds of 14/1. 1998 Melbourne Cup winning jockey Chris Munce hopped off Brew after the Saab win and partnered Metropolitan Handicap winner Coco Copana in the Cup.

Given plenty of time to mature, the six-year-old Brew was prepared by New Zealand trainer Michael Maroney, who also trained the third placegetter Second Coming in the 2000 Cup. Splitting the stablemates was the Brisbane Cup winner Yippyio, which had beaten Brew into fourth place in that race. Maroney later credited the Brisbane Winter campaign as the turning point in Brew's career.

Connections of Caulfield Cup winner Diatribe later lodged a formal protest over jockey Jim Cassidy's handling of the horse in the Melbourne Cup which, they alleged, were contrary to trainer George Hanlon's instructions.

Record Spot

Female trainer of the winner

2	Sheila Laxon (NZ)	Ethereal (2001)
	Gai Waterhouse (Australia)	Fiorente (2013)

* 'Granny' McDonald (NZ) was the trainer of 1938 winner Catalogue but the VRC did not recognise female trainers. Her husband, Mr A. McDonald, was registered as the trainer.

Did You Know

Sheila Laxon 'officially' became the first female trainer of a Melbourne Cup winner when Ethereal won in 2001. Of course, fellow New Zealander 'Granny' McDonald was the real trainer of 1938 winner Catalogue, but the VRC did not recognise female trainers (her husband, Mr A. McDonald, was registered as the trainer instead).

Sheila Laxon was the wife of Laurie Laxon, the trainer of 1988 Cup winner Empire Rose, before taking out her own training license in 1997. She later moved to Australia and set up a training partnership with John Symons in country Victoria

Gai Waterhouse, the daughter of champion Sydney trainer Tommy Smith, was the first Australian female trainer to win the Cup with Fiorente (2013). Waterhouse had enjoyed a series of placings in the Melbourne Cup (Te Akau Nick 1993; Nothin' Leica Dane 1995 and Fiorente 2012) before her success in 2013.

History Spot

Ethereal
(2001)

Ethereal's win in the 2001 Queensland Oaks (2400m) had to be seen to be believed. Ridden by local jockey Scott Seamer, the New Zealand filly came from a seemingly hopeless position to win in the last stride. A December foal, Ethereal had taken time to mature under the training of Shelia Laxon but the daughter of the classy Romani Coni was immediately set for the 'Big Cups' double later that year.

Ethereal ran three placings in New Zealand leading up to her Australian racing return in the Caulfield Cup. Reunited with Scott Seamer, Ethereal came with a withering burst to defeat the 1999 AJC Derby-Caulfield Cup winner Sky Heights by a head. The mare did not have another run before her Melbourne Cup success, in which she was penalised to carry 52kg, but trained to the minute Ethereal hauled in the internationals Give the Slip and Persian Punch to win by three quarters length.

New Zealand trainer Sheila Laxon had pulled off a rare double to officially become the first female trainer of a Melbourne Cup winner. A daughter of Rhythm (USA), Ethereal was simply a great mare. Her final race appearance produced an upset win over AJC Derby winner Universal Prince in the 2002 BMW Stakes.

Record Spot

Geelong Cup – Melbourne Cup

2002	Media Puzzle
2010	Americain
2011	Dunaden

Did You Know?

The Geelong Cup was rarely on the Melbourne Cup radar over the years, until international trainers started targeting the Group 3 race over 2400m in country Victoria, which is run 13 days before the Melbourne Cup. Realising the race afforded international horses a solid hit out under Australian handicap conditions, the Geelong Cup has since become an important piece of the Melbourne Cup form puzzle.

It was only fitting, then, that Irish visitor Media Puzzle threw down the gauntlet in the 2002 Melbourne Cup when he raced away at Geelong under the guidance of Damien Oliver. Bauer went within a lip of completing the double in 2008, before Americain (2010) and Dunaden (2011) followed the same path to success. Subsequent international Geelong Cup winners (Gatewood 2012, Ibicenco 2013, Caravan Rolls On 2014 and Almoonqith 2015) however, have just not been good enough to win the Melbourne Cup.

History Spot

Media Puzzle
(2002)

Almost a decade after becoming the first international trainer to win the Melbourne Cup with Vintage Crop, Irish trainer Dermot Weld won a second Cup with Media Puzzle in 2002. The entire nation, however, was diverted from the race by the tragedy that had engulfed the family of jockey Damien Oliver days before the Cup.

Oliver's brother Jason, also a jockey, was killed in a track fall the week before the Cup and it originally appeared that Damien would forfeit the ride. Given enough time to decide by Weld and his Australian mentor Lee Freedman, Oliver duly took the ride, won the Cup and dedicated the victory to his fallen brother.

It was the stuff of Hollywood movies – and it was later turned into one – but it was also a reality check for all racing fans about the dangers of horse racing. Oliver had previously suffered a broken back in a race fall and his father Ray was killed in a fall in the 1975 Kalgoorlie Cup.

Did You Know?

In The Cup (2011), the Simon Wincer-directed movie based on Damien Oliver's win on Media Puzzle in the 2002 Melbourne Cup, Oliver was played by actor Stephen Curry, trainer Dermot Weld was played by noted Irish actor Brendan Gleeson and Lee Freedman by Australian comic Shaun Micallef.

Record Spot

Multiple Cup Wins

3	Makybe Diva (2003, 2004, 2005)
2	Archer (1861, 1862)
2	Peter Pan (1932, 1934)
2	Rain Lover (1968, 1969)
2	Think Big (1974, 1975)

History Spot

Makybe Diva
(2003)

The biggest Melbourne Cup crowd recorded at Flemington – 122,736 people – saw mare Makybe Diva win the first of her record three Melbourne Cup victories in 2003. Bred in England by her millionaire owner Tony Santic, Makybe Diva (named after five women who worked in Santic's South Australian tuna fishery – Maureen, Kylie, Belinda, Diane and Vanesa) failed to sell as a yearling and was brought to Australia to race as a late three-year-old.

Trained by David Hall, Makybe Diva (Desert King –Tugela) ran fourth in a Benalla maiden before winning six races in succession in the Spring of 2002. The mare's wins in the Werribee Cup and Queen Elizabeth Stakes earmarked her as a future Cups hope by her connections. Her form leading up to the 2003 Melbourne Cup was solid enough – a series of four consecutive fourths in the Rundle Welter (1400m), Stock Stakes (1600m), Turnbull Stakes (2000m) and Caulfield Cup (2400m) – for her to start 8/1 second favourite in the Cup with just 51kg on her back.

Glen Boss rode Makybe Diva to a one and a half length win over the roughie She's Archie with Jardine's Lookout in third place. But the best was yet to come.

Opposite: The statue of Makybe Diva in Port Lincoln, South Australia, the home of the mare's owner-breeder Tony Santic.

143

Record Spot

Sydney Cup – Melbourne Cup

1890	Carbine
2004	Makybe Diva

Did You Know?

In capturing her second Melbourne Cup, Makybe Diva also became the first horse since the great Carbine to win the Sydney Cup–Melbourne Cup double in the same year. Having transferred to the Lee Freedman stable, Makybe Diva won the 2004 Sydney Cup after a long and previously winless Autumn campaign carrying 55.5kg, and was allotted the same weight for her second Melbourne Cup.

Makybe Diva was unlucky not to add a Caulfield Cup to her already imposing record when she ran the great Elvstroem to a head in the 2004 Caulfield Cup. The mare did not have another start before the Melbourne Cup, in which she was sent out a $3.60 favourite. On a heavy track, 'The Diva' defeated the top-weighted international by a length and a half, setting a weight-carrying record for a mare.

History Spot

Makybe Diva
(2005)

In 2005, Makybe Diva set several records in winning her third successive Melbourne Cup. The first top weight to win the Cup since Rising Fast in 1954, The Diva also set a weight-carrying record for a mare with 58kg, or 0.5kg over weight for age, breaking her own weight carrying record from the previous year (55.5kg).

Though deemed to be a seven-year-old under southern hemispheres conditions (Makybe Diva was actually foaled in March and was six months younger than the age group she raced in), The Diva was in the best form of her career in 2005. After winning the Australian Cup-BMW Stakes double in the Autumn, she returned in the Spring and was almost unbeatable – first in the Memsie Stakes (1400m), second in the Feehan Stakes (1600m), first in the Turnbull Stakes (2000m) and was an effortless winner of the Cox Plate (2040m).

In the Melbourne Cup, Glen Boss rode a supremely confident race down the centre of the track to win by two lengths as a $4.40 favourite. Successful trainer Lee Freedman told the press after his mare defeated On A Jeune and Xcellent: 'Go find the smallest child on this course, and there will be the only example of a person who will live long enough to see that again'.

Record Spot

Country where bred*

Australia	91	(Shocking 2009)
New Zealand	43	(Prince of Penzance 2015)
England	5	(Makybe Diva 2005)
USA	4	(Americain 2010)
Ireland	2	(Fiorente 2013)
Germany	2	(Protectionist 2014)
France	1	(Dunaden 2011)
Japan	1	(Delta Blues 2006)

Did You Know?

Delta Blues (2006) is the only Japanese-bred and trained horse to win the Melbourne Cup. Delta Blues was by the Japanese-based sire Dance in the Dark (by Sunday Silence USA) out of Dixie Splash (by Dixieland Band USA). In winning the 2006 Melbourne Cup, Delta Blues defeated another Japanese horse in Pop Rock, which was also trained by Katsuhiko Sumii. Yasunari Iwata became the first Japanese jockey to win the Cup when his mount defeated Pop Rock, ridden by local champion Damien Oliver, by a half-head.

Above: Delta Blues, ridden by Yasunari Iwata, holds off stablemate Pop Rock (Damien Oliver) to win the 2006 Melbourne Cup.

Record Spot

Victoria Derby winners which won the Melbourne Cup in a non-calendar year

	Victoria Derby	Melbourne Cup
Phar Lap	1929	1930
Comic Court	1948	1950
Delta	1949	1951
Efficient	2006	2007

Did You Know?

The VRC Derby has come in for a lot of criticism in recent years. Not only has no VRC Derby winner since Skipton (1941) gone on to win the Melbourne Cup in the same year, VRC Derby winners have had a very poor record in the Cup as older horses. Not surprisingly Phar Lap was the first to come back a year later and win the Cup as a four-year-old, while Comic Court and Delta came back two years after winning the Derby to win the Cups as five-year-olds.

The VRC Derby was first run in 1855 over 1½ miles (2400m). In 1973, the distance was extended to 2500m. Given that many Spring three-year-olds have not even celebrated their birthdays, some form analysts believe the race should be shortened to 2000m, but this is unlikely to happen.

History Spot

Efficient
(2007)

Even though it was a Melbourne Cup winner, Efficient may go down as one of the unluckiest horses in the modern era. A son of the all-conquering Zabeel, Efficient won five consecutive races as a Spring three-year-old in 2006 culminating in an easy, two and a half length win in the VRC Derby. Owner Lloyd Williams had such a high opinion of the colt that it was entered in the Melbourne Cup three days later but was scratched when the gelding had a poor recovery after the Derby run.

Efficient had a light Autumn program (two races) before being set for the 2007 Melbourne Cup. The grey was unplaced in four runs, including the WS Cox Plate, before carrying 54kg in the Cup. Ridden by Michael Rodd, the same jockey who had won the Derby the previous year, Efficient started at 16/1 and swept down the middle of the track to defeat international visitor Purple Moon by a half-length.

Efficient was trained by former New Zealand trainer Graeme Rogerson, but he soon parted ways with the owners after a less than gracious Cup acceptance speech. Trained by John Sadler, Efficient was scratched from both the 2008 and 2009 Melbourne Cup because of injury, and after winning the 2009 Turnbull Stakes spent over a year on the sidelines before running a close second in the 2011 Sydney Cup.

Record Spot

Brisbane Cup – Melbourne Cup

1959	Macdougal
2008	Viewed

Did You Know?

When Viewed won the Brisbane Cup in 2008 the distance had been reduced from 3200m to 2400m and downgraded to a Group 2 race. The reason for this could possibly have been the fact that the two-mile race was one of the last Group 1 events in the Australasian racing season and as such, has had little bearing on the Melbourne Cup over the years.

Queensland stayer Macdougal had been the only horse to complete the Brisbane Cup–Melbourne Cup double in the same year, in 1959. Two years before, Macdougal had shown promise by running third in the Brisbane Cup as a three-year-old. Viewed won the Brisbane Cup (2400m) by seven lengths on a bog track in 2008, which turned out to be as good a Cup trial as any.

Special mention must go to Yippyio, which won the Brisbane Cup in 2000 but failed to haul in Brew in the Melbourne Cup later that year, and Reckless (1977) which won the Sydney, Adelaide and Brisbane Cups but found one better in Gold and Black in the Melbourne Cup that year.

History Spot

Viewed

(2008)

Few punters gave Bart Cummins any chance of adding to his imposing Melbourne Cup record in the 2008 Cup. Having finished down the track in the Caulfield Cup, and then missed a run on Derby Day after a training setback, Cumming's main hope Viewed blew out to 40/1 in betting with stable followers pinning their hopes on the Lexus Stakes winner Moatize (12/1). The result? Never underestimate the Cups King's ability to get his horses ready on the first Tuesday in November.

Ridden by 21-year-old Blake Shin, Viewed surged to the front at the 300m mark – a little too early in Cummings' opinion – but held on from the Luca Cumani-trained Bauer in one of the closest photo finishes seen at Flemington. Viewed was owned by Cummings' long-term client Dato' Tan Chin Nam, who had been the successful owner in Think Big (1974–75) and Saintly (1996).

Viewed returned the following year to win the Caulfield Cup before running seventh to Shocking in the 2009 Melbourne Cup. The following year, the six-year-old stallion had to be euthanised following complications from a twisted bowel.

The finish to the 2008 Melbourne Cup was so close that the electronic timing devices, which are placed inside the saddle cloths, recorded that Bauer actually completed the 3200m course one-hundredth of a second faster than Viewed but had still run second in the photo finish.

Record Spot

Lexus Stakes (Hotham Hcp) - Melbourne Cup

1922	King Ingoda	1931	White Nose
1943	Dark Felt	1944	Sirius
1949	Foxzami	1958	Baystone
1974	Think Big	2000	Brew
2009	Shocking		

Did You Know?

The Hotham Handicap, now called the Lexus Stakes, is the last chance for many lightly weighted or non-qualified horses to gain a place in the Melbourne Cup. Conducted under handicap conditions on Derby Day over 2500m, the race has invariably thrown up a Melbourne Cup winner, with Brew (2000) and Shocking (2009) earning their place in the Cup with a win on the Saturday and then going on to win the big race on Tuesday.

The Hotham Handicap was inaugurated in 1869 (1½ miles or 2400m) and underwent several name changes in the 1980s and 1990s before settling into its present incarnation. King Ingoda (1922) was the first Hotham Handicap–Melbourne Cup winner, but given the race's status as a legitimate Cup guide, the race has still only yielded eight Melbourne Cup winners over 155 years – an average of just one every 20 years!

Maluckyday (2010), Maybe Better (2006), Sea Legend (1986), Chagemar (1984) and Karu (1979) have all ran Melbourne Cup placings after winning the 'Last Chance' Stakes on the Saturday, but the double continues to be elusive.

Americain
(2010)

The 150th running of the Melbourne Cup presented Bart Cummings with his best chance to add to his record 12 Cup wins when the veteran trainer saddled up the short-priced favourite So You Think. The four-year-old son of High Chaparral had won the past two Cox Plates at WFA and was undefeated during the Spring, but was tackling the Melbourne Cup at only its eleventh start in a race.

On a slow track over two exhausting miles, however, Americain become the first French-trained horse to win the race, and Gerald Mosse the first French jockey. So You Think was a tiring third, with Maluckyday splitting the pair. Although trained by Alain de Royer Dupre in France Americain, as the name suggested, was USA-bred, by Dynaformer (like At Talaq, a son of Roberto) out of the Arazi mare America.

So You Think was sold to Coolmore Stud after his Melbourne Cup defeat – denying the horse the chance to win the Cup as a five-year-old, but he raced successfully in Europe before being retired to stud. Americain ran a good fourth in the 2011 Melbourne Cup, and then captured the Sandown Classic (2400m) before later being retired to stud in Australia.

Record Spot

The Greatest Melbourne Cup Never Run (2010)

To mark the 150th running of the Melbourne Cup in 2010, Racing Victoria's handicapper Greg Carpenter ranked the greatest Cup winners from 1–24. Carpenter did the hard work for the panel of 22 experts, who determined that the top four horses on the list would have finished the 'phantom' Melbourne Cup in that order given the compressed weight scale that was framed – Phar Lap first, followed by Carbine and Makybe Diva, with Peter Pan fourth.

For the sake of an argument, I would have found a place for Gold and Black (1977) at the expense of Hall Mark (1933). Only Makybe Diva (58kg) and Think Big (58.5kg) have carried more weight that Gold and Black did in 1977 (57kg) to win the Cup in the 'metric' era. Hall Mark won the Cup with a three-year-old's weight advantage and only beat Shadow King. Gold and Black beat Reckless and probably should have won two Melbourne Cups.

1.	PHAR LAP (Jim Pike) Harry Telford	60kg	(1930)
2.	CARBINE (Bob Ramage) Walter Hickenbotham	59kg	(1890)
3.	MAKYBE DIVA (Glen Boss) Lee Freedman	58kg	(2003-05)
4.	PETER PAN (Darby Munro) Frank McGrath	58kg	(1932, 1934)
5.	GALILEE (John Miller) Bart Cummings	57.5kg	(1966)
6.	POSEIDON (Tom Clayton) Ike Earnshaw	57.5kg	(1906)
7.	RISING FAST (Jack Purtell) Ivan Tucker	57kg	(1954)
8.	RAIN LOVER (Jim Johnson) Mick Robins	56kg	(1968-69)
9.	COMIC COURT (Pat Glennon) Jim Cummings	55.5kg	(1950)
10.	GRAND FLANEUR (Tom Hales) Tom Brown	55.5kg	(1880)
11.	MIGHT AND POWER (Jim Cassidy) Jack Denham	55kg	(1997)
12.	ARCHER (Johnny Cutts) Etienne De Mestre	54kg	(1861-62)
13.	VINTAGE CROP (Mick Kinane) Dermot Weld	54kg	(1993)
14.	DELTA (Neville Sellwood) Maurice McCarten	53.5kg	(1951)
15.	MALUA (Alick Robertson) Isaac Foulsham	53.5kg	(1884)
16.	NIGHTMARCH (Roy Reed) Alex McAulay	53.5kg	(1929)
17.	POITREL (Ken Bracken) Harry Robinson	53.5kg	(1920)
18.	SAINTLY (Darren Beadman) Bart Cummings	53kg	(1996)
19.	THE BARB (William Davis) John Tait	53kg	(1866)
20.	DALRAY (Bill Williamson) Clarrie McCarthy	52.5kg	(1952)
21.	HALL MARK (Jack O'Sullivan) Jack Holt	52.5kg	(1933)
22.	LIGHT FINGERS (Roy Higgins) Bart Cummings	52.5kg	(1965)
23.	DORIEMUS (Damien Oliver) Lee Freedman	52kg	(1995)

History Spot

Dunaden
(2011)

Dunaden became the first French-bred horse (Nicobar-La Marlia), and the second French-trained horse (Mikel Delzangles), to win the Melbourne Cup when it literally defeated Red Cadeaux by a whisker in 2011. Using state of the art digital technology, the judge was able to distinguish that Dunaden had won the Cup by a matter of millimetres from the luckless Red Cadeaux. Before the advent of computer technology, this result in any other era would have been deemed a dead heat – a Melbourne Cup first!

Dunaden went on to win the prestigious Hong Kong Vase a few weeks later with Red Cadeaux running a good third. The following year, Dunaden won the Caulfield Cup at its first run back in Australia but was unplaced in Green Moon's Melbourne Cup after carrying top weight of 59kg. Red Cadeaux was also unplaced in the 2012 Cup, but came back to run seconds in successive years (2013 and 2014).

Did You Know?

The only dead heat in Melbourne Cup history has been for third place. Zazabelle and Lahar dead-heated in 1999, while Gaine Carrington and Topical dead-heated for third in 1933.

Green Moon
(2012)

Few owners have more of a fascination with the Melbourne Cup than businessman and property developer Lloyd Williams (born 1940). Williams was a close businesses associate of the late media mogul Kerry Packer, Australia's richest man, and founded Melbourne's Crown Casino before selling his interests to Packer's son, James Packer.

Williams was the co-owner of previous Cup winners Just a Dash (1981), What a Nuisance (1985) and Efficient (2007). Irish-bred Green Moon (Montjeu-Noon) was purchased by Williams with the express purpose of winning the Melbourne Cup in 2011, but failed to qualify for the race that year despite winning the Newcastle Gold Cup and running second in the Caulfield Cup.

A year later, Green Moon won the Turnbull Stakes (2000m) and started favourite for the WS Cox Plate, but an unplaced run saw the Robert Hickmott-trained Entire drift to 20/1 on Cup Day. Ridden by Brett Pebble, Green Moon held out fellow internationals Fiorente and Jakkalberry to win, leaving former Cup winners Dunaden and Americain in its wake.

History Spot

Fiorente
(2013)

Sydney trainer Gai Waterhouse, the daughter of champion trainer Tommy Smith, became the first Australian female trainer to win the Melbourne Cup in 2013. Waterhouse was successful with the Irish-bred import Fiorente, which had run such a great second to Green Moon the previous year. Fiorente started $7 favourite on the strength of the horse's good third in the WS Cox Plate, and was ridden by premier Melbourne jockey Damien Oliver.

Red Cadeaux was a surprise second, after the 2011 runner-up's unplaced run the previous year, with Mount Athos third. Fiorente returned in the Autumn with a win in the Australian Cup (2000m) before breaking down and being retired to stud.

Did You Know?

Bill McLachlan, Darby Munro, Jack Purtell, Jimmy Johnson, Damien Oliver and Glen Boss have won three cups each. Oliver and Boss, however, can improve on their records and equal or surpass the record jointly held by Bobby Lewis and Harry White (4 each). Oliver has also ridden close seconds on Paris Lane (1994), Pop Rock (2006) and Purple Moon (2007).

Protectionist
(2014)

B red in Germany, Protectionist was owned by an Australian syndicate and trained by Andreas Wöhler. The son of Monsun, the same sire as 2013 Cup winner Fiorente, won two races during his four-year-old season before coming to Australia in the Spring of 2014. Protectionist's only start in Australia before its Cup success was a slashing fourth in the Herbert Power Handicap, carrying 59kg.

Australian jockey Craig Williams rode Protectionist in the Herbert Power, but was subsequently suspended and replaced by English rider Ryan Moore for the Melbourne Cup. Protectionist won the race easily by four lengths, in what was only its tenth career start, with the luckless Red Cadeaux second and Who Shot the Barman third. Protectionist remained in Australia to be trained by Kris Lees, but could not recapture its best form and was returned to Germany where it won a second Hansa-Preis (2400m).

Two horses had to be put down after 2014 Cup, including favourite Admire Rakti, which was carrying the heaviest weight since Think Big (1975), and finished with a distressed last. The Japanese-trained Caulfield Cup winner died of heart failure in his stall. Araldo broke his leg and had to be euthanised after being spooked by a large flag being waved in the crowd after the race.

Bart Cummings

Bart Cummings' career record in the Melbourne Cup (1958–2014)
'Cups King' Bart Cummings passed away on 30 August 2015, aged 87. His final runner in the Melbourne Cup was Precedence, which he trained in partnership with his grandson James Cummings. Precedence failed to make the final field in 2015 Melbourne Cup, bringing to a close Cummings' record-breaking history in the great race.

1958	Asian Court (12th)
1959	Trellios (5th)
1961	Sometime (6th)
1965	Light Fingers (WON), Ziema (2nd), The Dip (18th)
1966	Galilee (WON), Light Fingers (2nd)
1967	(Red Handed WON), Fulmen, (9th), Ziema (12th)
1968	Lowland (4th), Arctic Coast (6th), Galilee (8th), Swift General (23rd).
1969	Swift General (5th), General Command, (13th), The Sharper (20th)
1970	Tavel (4th), Voleur (6th), Moomba Fox (19th)
1971	Pilgarlic (10th), Tavel (19th)
1973	Dayana (12th)
1974	Think Big (WON), Leilani (2nd)
1975	Think Big (WON), Holiday Waggon (2nd), Leica Lover (20th)
1976	Gold and Black (2nd)
1977	Gold and Black (WON), Ming Dynasty (8th), Vacuum (20th)
1978	Panamint (10th), Vive Velours (11th), Belmura Lad (13th), Stormy Rex (20th)
1979	Hyperno (WON), Safe Harbour (21st)
1980	La Zap (6th), Hyperno (7th), Ming Dynasty (17th)

Year	Results
1981	Hyperno (6th), Belmura Lad (7th), No Peer (8th)
1982	My Sir Avon (4th)
1983	Mr Jazz (3rd), No Peer (4th):
1984	Bounty Hawk (15th)
1986	Empire Rose (5th)
1987	Rosedale (3rd)
1988	Round the World (5th)
1990	Kingston Rule (WON), La Tristia (9th)
1991	Let's Elope (WON), Shiva's Revenge (2nd), Weekend Delight (22nd)
1992	London Bridge (9th)
1993	Great Vintage (4th), Frontier Boy (5th), Tennessee Jack (6th), Our Tristalight (24th)
1994	Gossips (14th)
1996	Saintly (WON), My Kiwi Gold (21st)
1997	Grandmaster (10th), Alfa (19th)
1998	Perpetual Check (9th)
1999	Rogan Josh (WON), Zazabelle (3rd), Rebbor (23rd)
2002	Miss Meliss (10th)
2003	Frightening (11th)
2004	Strasbourg (10th)
2005	Kamsky (16th), Strasbourg (18th)
2007	Sirmione (12th)
2008	Viewed (WON), Moatize (6th)
2009	Viewed (7th), Allez Wonder (16th), Roman Emperor (21st)
2010	So You Think (3rd), Precedence (8th)
2011	Precedence (11th), Illo (19th)
2012	Precedence (9th), Sanagas (18th)
2014	Precedence (6th)

Record Spot

Successful female jockeys

1	Michelle Payne (Prince of Penzance, 2015)

Female Jockeys in the Melbourne Cup

1987	New Zealander Maree Lyndon was the first woman to ride in a Melbourne Cup, finishing 20th on Argonaut Style.
2003	The first Australian female jockey to ride in the cup was Clare Lindop on Debben.
2007	Two female jockeys ride in a Melbourne Cup for the first time. Clare Lindop rides Dolphin Jo into 5th place while Lisa Cropp finishes 9th on Sculptor.
2009	Michelle Payne finishes 16th on the Bart Cummings-trained Allez Wonder.

Did You Know?

In the 2015 Melbourne Cup, the only Australian-bred horse to start in the race was Sertorious (Galileo – Pretty Penny,) which finished in the middle of the field. The other 23 horses that made the final field comprised seven bred in Great Britain, six from Ireland, five from New Zealand, two from Japan, and one each from Germany, USA and France.

Prince of Penzance
(2015)

Michelle Payne became the first female jockey to win the Cup when Prince of Penzance won at 100/1 in 2015. Payne rode a masterful race and timed her run to perfection in surging the six-year-old Entire gelding to the front at the 100m mark. Prince of Penzance defeated Max Dynamite (Frankie Dettori) and the AJC Derby winner Criterion (Michael Walker), with most observers believing Payne outrode both international jockeys.

Prince of Penzance was trained by Darren Weir for a large syndicate of owners. Michael Payne is the youngest daughter of the well-known horse racing Payne family, with younger brother Stevie drawing the number 1 barrier at the official barrier draw. Prince of Penzance won the Mooney Valley Cup in 2014, and backed up a year later to run a good second to The United States in its final lead up race for the Cup. Payne, who some of the owners wanted to replace in the Cup, repaid the faith shown in her by trainer Weir and gave a royal 'get stuffed' to those who doubted the ability of female jockeys to win major races.

Tragically, three-time runner-up Red Cadeaux did not finish the race in its fifth Cup start after suffering a fetlock injury for which the nine-year-old gelding was later euthanised.

Appendices
Odds & Sods

Gambling

The Melbourne Cup is not only the race that stops a nation, but it also propels the nation to spend millions of dollars to find the eventual winner. From professional gamblers to once a year punters, it is in the DNA of the Australian public to have a 'flutter' on the first Tuesday in November. People who have never gambled in their lives back horses for a win, place or each-way and in quinellas, exactas, trifectas and 'first fours.'

In 2015, a combined $300 million dollars was wagered on the race, or $12.50 for every man, woman and child in the country. The days of visiting the friendly SP bookie down the road are well and truly over, so bets are placed at the local TAB, on line with corporate bookmakers or with on course bookies at hundreds of tracks around the country.

Odds

The chance of each of the 24 horses winning the race is 1 in 24 (or 24/1) on paper, but this does not take into account ability, form, weight, age, sex, barrier, jockey and trainer. Bookmakers take these factors into account and adjust the odds accordingly ... the 'favourite runner' might start at 4/1 and 'outsider' horses ('no hopes') at 100/1 or 200/1.

Once a year punters have been known to back every horse in the race so that they can have bragging rights for the next year that they 'backed the winner of the Cup'. Of course, to finish with more money than you invested the winner has to pay more than $24, which has happened only twice since 2000 (Viewed 2008 and Prince of Penzance 2015). Last year, Prince of Penzance started at 101/1 at fixed odds on the TAB, so you would have finished $77 in the black.

In the early 1990s, bookmakers odds were finally decimalised by the TAB, bringing an end to the era of 6/4 favourites and 11/2 each way hopes. It actually took a lot of the fun out of battling with the bookies for old punters and having them convert the wager into a win bet ('That's $25 at 6/4 for a return of $62.50, thanks champ,' they would say quick as a flash as they wrote the ticket).

For old time's sake, here's a quick explanation of how the 'odds' used to work:

'Odds on' means you risk more money than you win (e.g. 2/1 on = $1.50 including your $1 stake)

'Even money': invest $1 = $2 return*

10/9 = $2.10	5/4 = $2.25	11/8 = $2.35	6/4 = $2.50	13/8= $2.60	7/4 = $2.75
15/8 = $2.85	2/1 = $3.00	9/4 = $3.25	5/2 = $3.50	11/4 = $3.75	3/1 = $4.00
13/4 = $4.25	7/2 = $4.50	15/4 = $4.25	4/1 = $5.00	9/2 = $5.50	5/1 = $6.00
11/2 = $6.50	6/1 = $7.00	13/2 =$7.50	7/1 = $8.00	15/2 = $8.50	8/1 = $9.00

*including your stake

Quinella

To back the 'quinella' in the race, you have to pick first and second in any order. Bart Cummings, of course was not only the 'Cup's King' but also the 'Quinella King', training first and second on a record five occasions (1965–66, 1974–75 and 1991). When Lee Freedman trained first and second place in 1989, younger brother Richard famously quipped 'we've done a 'Bart Cummings!' Japanese trainer Katsuhiko Sumii achieved the same feat in 2006 with Delta Blues and Pop Rock.

To cover every horse in the race you would have to multiple 24 horses by 23 horses and then halve it (quinellas can be in any order, remember). This means there are 276 combinations in a full Melbourne Cup field of 24. Punters who were game enough to invest $276 on the quinella in 2015 would have received a dividend of $794 (Prince of Penzance/Max Dynamite) for a tidy profit of $508.

The box six horses in the quinella costs $15 (6 x 5 divided by 2) for a 100 per cent dividend.

Exacta

The exacta is a form of quinella where you have to pick first and second in the exact order that they finish. Because of this, most punters 'box' their selections so that they can finish in any order, but this means you have to invest twice as much as a quinella. To box all the runners in a Melbourne Cup would cost $552 (24 x 23). In 2015, the exacta paid $1770 (for a tidy profit of $1218) but then a $101 winner puts a lot of value into the dividend.

To box six horses in the exacta costs $30 (6 x 5) for a 100% dividend.

Trifecta

The trifecta asks punters to select the first three horses across the line in the correct order. Because this is a herculean task in any race, let alone a 24-field Melbourne Cup, most punters box their selections so they can finish in any order. This costs $6 (3 x 2 x 1) for a 100% dividend, although punters can opt for any percentage of this (e.g. $3 box trifecta = 50% dividend).

To box all the combinations in a Melbourne Cup would cost $12,144 (24 x 23 x 22), meaning there are more than 12,000 available combinations. In 2015, the trifecta paid $20,010 – for a nice profit of almost $8,000 – but I don't suggest you try it unless you have deep pockets!

To box six horses in the trifecta costs $120 (6 x 5 x 4) for a 100% dividend.

First Four

The 'first four' is exactly what it says ... picking the first four horses across the line in any given race. In the capacity field of the Melbourne Cup, however, that would cost more than a quarter of a million dollars (24 x 23 x 22 x 21 = $255,024 for a 100 per cent). In 2015, the First Four on the Melbourne Cup paid $307,081 for a profit of about $52,000. Risking $250,000 to win $52,000 is not a good investment given the first four rarely pays over $100,000.

To box six horses in the 'first four' costs a hefty $720 (6 x 5 x 4 x 3) for a 100% dividend. If this is too prohibitive, boxing five horses costs $120 (5 x 4 x 3 x 2) and boxing four horses costs just $24.

HOW TO PICK THE WINNER OF THE MELBOURNE CUP!

Last Start Form Guide for Cup Winners since 2000

2015	Prince of Penzance	MOONEY VALLEY CUP (2nd)
2014	Protectionist	HERBERT POWER HCP (4th)
2013	Fiorente	WS COX PLATE (3rd)
2012	Green Moon	WS COX PLATE (7th)
2011	Dunaden	GEELONG CUP (1st)
2010	Americain	GEELONG CUP (1st)
2009	Shocking	LEXUS STAKES (1st)
2008	Viewed	CAULFIELD CUP (10th)
2007	Efficient	WS COX PLATE (9th)
2006	Delta Blues	CAULFIELD CUP (3rd)
2005	Makybe Diva	WS COX PLATE (1st)
2004	Makybe Diva	CAULFIELD CUP (5th)
2003	Makybe Diva	CAULFIELD CUP (4th)
2002	Media Puzzle	GEELONG CUP (1st)
2001	Ethereal	CAULFIELD CUP (1st)
2000	Brew	LEXUS STAKES (1st)

In the modern era, the Caulfield Cup and Cox Plate remain the best guides to finding the Melbourne Cup winner. Look for horse that place or run on in either race. The Geelong Cup remains the favoured pathway to the race for international horses but the winner must win with some authority. The Lexus (winner only) and the Mooney Valley Cup (placegetters) have also produced a winner.

It is interesting to note that unexposed form by the international horses

does not translate to success in the Cup – since 1993, no international raider has won the Melbourne Cup 'first up' although Max Dynamite (2nd in 2015), Red Cadeuax (2nd in 2011, 2013–14), Crime Scene (2nd in 2009), Purple Moon (2nd in 2007), Pop Rock (2nd in 2007) Vinnie Roe (2nd in 2004), Give the Slip (2nd in 2001) and Central Park (2nd in 1999) went close.

The only winners which don't fit the pattern in this period are Protectionist in 2014 (it would have been interesting to see what would have happened if Protectionist had started in the Geelong Cup) and Prince of Penzance, which used the Mooney Valley Cup as a lead-up race. The Mooney Valley Cup will come increasingly into play as a form guide now the LKS Mackinnon Stakes had been moved to after the Melbourne Cup.

THE BLACK BOOK
Picking the Winner of the Cup

2015 Caulfield Cup (2400m):

1. Mongolian Khan* 2. Trip to Paris
3. Our Ivanhowe 4. Gust of Wind

2015 Mooney Valley Cup (2600m): 1. United States 2. Prince of Penzance (WON)

2015 Geelong Cup (2400m): 1. Almoonquith

2015 WS Cox Plate (2050m): 1. Winx* 2. Criterion (3rd) * Did not run in the Cup

2015 Lexus Stakes (2500m): 1. Excess Knowledge

In trying to find the winner of future Melbourne Cups, try this formula for filtering the 24 runners:

2016 Caulfield Cup:
Do not include the Caulfield Cup winner because the horse is invariably weighted out of the Melbourne Cup.

2. _____
3. _____
4. _____

2016 Mooney Valley Cup:

1. _____
2. _____

2016 Geelong Cup:

1. _____ (winner only)

2016 Cox Plate:
Include third horse if winner doesn't start in the Melbourne Cup.

1. _____
2/3. _____

2016 Lexus Stakes

1. _____ (winner only)

This should narrow the field of 24 down to about 6–8 chances, so the rest is up to you!

My Selections: _____

_____

2017 Caulfield Cup: 2. _____

3. _____

4. _____

2017 Mooney Valley Cup: 1. _____

2. _____

2017 Geelong Cup: 1. _____ (winner only)

2017 Cox Plate: 1. _____

2/3. _____

2017 Lexus Stakes   1. _____ (winner only)

This should narrow the field of 24 down to about 6-8 chances, so the rest is up to you!

My Selections: _____

_____

2018 Caulfield Cup: 2. _____

3. _____

4. _____

2018 Mooney Valley Cup: 1. _____

2. _____

2018 Geelong Cup: 1. _____ (winner only)

2018 Cox Plate: 1. _____

2/3. _____

2018 Lexus Stakes   1. _____ (winner only)

This should narrow the field of 24 down to about 6-8 chances, so the rest is up to you!

My Selections: _____

_____

YEAR	WINNER	AGE SEX	JOCKEY	TRAINER	OWNER	TIME
2016						
2015	Prince of Penzance	6 g	Michelle Payne	Darren Weir	A.McGregor, A.T. Broadfoot, Galadi Holdings, Wilawl Go Racing Synd, Dalton Racing, Men In Hats Synd, Winning Five Synd	3:23.15
2014	Protectionist	5 h	Ryan Moore	Andreas Wöhler	Christoph Berglar, Australian Bloodstock	3:17.71
2013	Fiorente	6 h	Damien Oliver	Gai Waterhouse	Andrew Roberts and 39 others	3:20.30
2012	Green Moon	6 h	Brett Prebble	Robert Hickmott	Lloyd Williams	3:20.45
2011	Dunaden	6 h	Christophe Lemaire	Mikel Delzangles	Pearl Bloodstock Pty (Mgr. R Levitt)	3:20.84
2010	Americain	6 h	Gérald Mossé	Alain de Royer-Dupre	Gerry Ryan, K. C Bamford	3:26.87
2009	Shocking	4 h	Corey Brown	Mark Kavanagh	Eales Racing Pty Ltd	3:23.87
2008	Viewed	5 h	Blake Shinn	Bart Cummings	Tan Chin Nam, et al.	3:20.40
2007	Efficient	4 g	Michael Rodd	Graeme Rogerson	Lloyd Williams et al.	3:23.34
2006	Delta Blues	6 h	Yasunari Iwata	Katsuhiko Sumii	Sunday Racing Co Ltd	3:21.47
2005	Makybe Diva	7 m	Glen Boss	Lee Freedman	Emily Krstina Syndicate	3:19.17
2004	Makybe Diva	6 m	Glen Boss	Lee Freedman	Emily Krstina Syndicate	3:28.55
2003	Makybe Diva	5 m	Glen Boss	David Hall	Emily Krstina Syndicate	3:19.90
2002	Media Puzzle	6 g	Damien Oliver	Dermot K. Weld	Dr M. W. Smurfit, et al.	3:16.97
2001	Ethereal	4 m	Scott Seamer	Sheila Laxon	P. J. & P. M. Vela	3:21.08
2000	Brew	6 g	Kerrin McEvoy	Mike Moroney	Gurner's Bloodstock Co.	3:18.68

Year	Horse	Age/Sex	Jockey	Trainer	Owner	Time
1999	Rogan Josh	7 g	John Marshall	Bart Cummings	Mrs W. L. Green, et al.	3:19.64
1998	Jezabeel	6 m	Chris Munce	Brian Jenkins	A. K. Burr, et al.	3:18.59
1997	Might and Power	4 h	Jim Cassidy	Jack Denham	Mr N. Moraitis	3:18.33
1996	Saintly	4 g	Darren Beadman	Bart Cummings	Dato Tan Chin Nam, et al.	3:18.80
1995	Doriemus	5 g	Damien Oliver	Lee Freedman	Pacers Australia Syndicate	3:27.60
1994	Jeune	6 h	Wayne Harris	David Hayes	Shadwell Racing	3:19.80
1993	Vintage Crop	7 g	Michael Kinane	Dermot K. Weld	Dr M. W. Smurfit	3:23.40
1992	Subzero	4 h	Greg Hall	Lee Freedman	D H K Investments	3:24.70
1991	Let's Elope	4 m	Steven King	Bart Cummings	Shoreham Park Syndicate	3:18.90
1990	Kingston Rule	5 h	Darren Beadman	Bart Cummings	Mr & Mrs D. H. Hains	3:16.30
1989	Tawrrific	5 h	Shane Dye	Lee Freedman	B. F. Avery, et al.	3:17.10
1988	Empire Rose	6 m	Tony Allan	Laurie Laxon	Mr & Mrs F. R. Bodle	3:18.90
1987	Kensei	5 g	Larry Olsen	Les J. Bridge	K. M. Mitchell, et al.	3:22.00
1986	At Talaq	6 h	Michael Clarke	C S Hayes	Shadwell Racing	3:21.70
1985	What A Nuisance	7 g	Pat Hyland	John Meagher	Lloyd & Suzy Williams	3:23.00
1984	Black Knight	5 g	Peter Cook	George Hanlon	Robert Holmes à Court	3:18.90
1983	Kiwi	6 g	Jim Cassidy	Ewen S. Lupton	Mr & Mrs E. S. Lupton	3:18.90
1982	Gurner's Lane	4 g	Mick Dittman	Geoff T. Murphy	Williams St. Syndicate No 2	3:21.20
1981	Just A Dash	4 g	Peter Cook	T J Smith	Lloyd J. Williams, et al.	3:21.20
1980	Beldale Ball	5 h	John Letts	C S Hayes	Swettenham Stud Syndicate	3:19.80
1979	Hyperno	6 g	Harry White	Bart Cummings	Mr & Mrs T. L. North, et al.	3:21.80

YEAR	WINNER	AGE SEX	JOCKEY	TRAINER	OWNER	TIME
1978	Arwon	5 g	Harry White	George Hanlon	Doon Bros Syndicate & B Wakefield, R Wilson, J Watson	3:24.30
1977	Gold and Black	5 g	John Duggan	Bart Cummings	Mr & Mrs J. Harris, et al.	3:18.40
1976	Van der Hum	5 g	Robert J. Skelton	Len H. Robinson	L. H. & R. A. Robinson, et al.	3:34.10
1975	Think Big	5 g	Harry White	Bart Cummings	Tan Chin Nam, et al.	3:29.60
1974	Think Big	4 g	Harry White	Bart Cummings	Tan Chin Nam, et al.	3:23.10
1973	Gala Supreme	4 g	Frank Reys	Ray J. Hutchins	J. P. Curtain	3:19.50
1972	Piping Lane	6 g	John Letts	George Hanlon	R. W. Trinder	3:19.30
1971	Silver Knight	4 h	R. Bruce Marsh	Eric Temperton	Sir W. Norwood	3:19.50
1970	Baghdad Note	5 g	Midge Didham	Robert Heasley	E. C. S. Falconer	3:19.70
1969	Rain Lover	5 h	Jim Johnson	Mick L. Robins	Clifford A. Reid	3:21.50
1968	Rain Lover	4 h	Jim Johnson	Mick L. Robins	Clifford A. Reid	3:19.10
1967	Red Handed	5 g	Roy Higgins	Bart Cummings	F. W. Clarke, et al.	3:20.40
1966	Galilee	4 g	John Miller	Bart Cummings	Mr & Mrs M. L. Bailey	3:21.90
1965	Light Fingers	4 m	Roy Higgins	Bart Cummings	W. J. Broderick	3:21.10
1964	Polo Prince	6 g	Ron Taylor	John P. Carter	Mr & Mrs L. W. Davis	3:19.60
1963	Gatum	5 g	Jim Johnson	H. Graeme Heagney	M. P. Reid	3:21.10
1962	Even Stevens	5 h	Les Coles	Arch McGregor	James Wattie	3:21.40
1961	Lord Fury	4 h	Ray Selkrig	Frank B. Lewis	Mr & Mrs N. S. Cohen	3:19.50
1960	Hi Jinx	5 m	William A. Smith	Trevor H. Knowles	T. H. Knowles & K. R. Sly	3:23.75

Year	Horse	Age	Jockey	Trainer	Owner	Time
1959	Macdougal	6 g	Pat Glennon	Richard W. Roden	R. N. & N. H. B. Brown	3:23.00
1958	Baystone	6 g	Mel Schumacher	Jack Green	R. A. & N. Burns	3:21.25
1957	Straight Draw	5 g	Noel L. McGrowdie	J. M. Mitchell	Ezra Norton	3:24.50
1956	Evening Peal	4 m	George Podmore	E. D. Lawson	Mr & Mrs R. White	3:19.50
1955	Toparoa	7 g	Neville Sellwood	T J Smith	N. H. McDonald	3:28.25
1954	Rising Fast	5 g	Jack Purtell	Ivan Tucker	L. R. Spring	3:23.00
1953	Wodalla	4 h	Jack Purtell	Robert Sinclair	E. A. 'Ted' Underwood	3:23.75
1952	Dalray	4 h	Bill Williamson	C. C. McCarthy	C. Neville	3:23.75
1951	Delta	5 h	Neville Sellwood	Maurice McCarten	Adolph Basser	3:24.25
1950	Comic Court	5 h	Pat Glennon	J. M. Cummings	R. A., J. D. & A. J. Lee	3:19.50
1949	Foxzami	4 h	William Fellows	D. Lewis	L. G. Robinson	3:28.50
1948	Rimfire	6 g	Ray Neville	Stan Boyden	H. G. Raymond	3:21.00
1947	Hiraji	4 g	Jack Purtell	J. W. McCurley	Fred W. Hughes	3:28.00
1946	Russia	6 h	Darby Munro	E. Hush	J. G. Leeds & E. Hush	3:21.25
1945	Rainbird	4 m	Billy Cook	S. Evans	Clifford A. Reid	3:24.25
1944	Sirius	4 h	Darby Munro	E. Fisher	R.Turnbull	3:24.50
1943	Dark Felt	6 h	Vic Hartney	Ray Webster	J. A. Cain	3:23.25
1942	Colonus	4 h	H. McCloud	F. Manning	L. O. Menck	3:33.25
1941	Skipton	3 c	Billy Cook	J. Fryer	J. J. Kitson	3:23.75
1940	Old Rowley	7 g	Andy Knox	J. A. Scully	J. A. Scully	3:26.00
1939	Rivette	6 m	Teddy Preston	Harry Bamber	Harry Bamber	3:27.00

YEAR	WINNER	AGE SEX	JOCKEY	TRAINER	OWNER	TIME
1938	Catalogue	8 g	F. Shean	Allan McDonald	Mrs. A. Jamieson	3:26.25
1937	The Trump	5 g	Ashley Reed	S. W. Reid	E. Eccles	3:21.50
1936	Wotan	4 h	Ossie Phillips	J. Fryer	T. A., W. & R. Smith	3:21.25
1935	Marabou	4 h	K. Voitre	Lou Robertson	J. Fell & T. Hogan	3:23.75
1934	Peter Pan	5 h	Darby Munro	Frank McGrath Sr.	Rodney R. Dangar	3:40.50
1933	Hall Mark	3 c	J. O'Sullivan	Jack Holt	C. B. Kellow	3:27.50
1932	Peter Pan	3 c	Bill Duncan	Frank McGrath, Sr.	Rodney R. Dangar	3:23.25
1931	White Nose	5 h	N. Percival	E. J. Hatwell	H. P. McLachlan	3:26.00
1930	Phar Lap	4 g	James E. Pike	Harry R. Telford	Harry R. Telford and David J. Davis	3:27.75
1929	Nightmarch	4 h	Roy Reed	A. McAulay	A. Louisson	3:26.50
1928	Statesman	4 h	James L. Munro	William Kelso	William Kelso	3:23.25
1927	Trivalve	3 c	Bobby Lewis	James Scobie	E. E. D. Clarke	3:24.00
1926	Spearfelt	5 h	Hugh Harold Cairns	V. O'Neill	D. C. Grant	3:22.75
1925	Windbag	4 h	James L. Munro	George R. Price	R. Miller	3:22.75
1924	Backwood	6 h	Bunty Brown	Richard Bradfield	E. Baillieu, et al.	3:26.50
1923	Bitalli	5 g	Alan 'Titch' Wilson	James Scobie	A. T. Craig	3:24.25
1922	King Ingoda	4 h	Alan 'Titch' Wilson	James Scobie	C.L. Dubois/R.W. Bennett	3:28.25
1921	Sister Olive	3 f	Ted O'Sullivan	J. Williams	F. W. Norman	3:27.75
1920	Poitrel	6 h	Ken Bracken	H. J. Robinson	W. & F. A. Moses	3:25.75
1919	Artilleryman	3 c	Bobby Lewis	P. T. Heywood	Sir S. Hordern/A.D. Murphy	3:24.50

Year	Horse		Jockey	Trainer	Owner	Time
1918	Night Watch	5 g	Bill Duncan	Richard Bradfield	C. L. Macdonald	3:25.75
1917	Westcourt	5 h	William McLachlan	Joe Burton	D. U. Seaton	3:26.75
1916	Sasanof	3 g	F. Foley	M. Hobbs	W.G. Stead/E.S. Luttrell	3:27.75
1915	Patrobas	3 c	Bobby Lewis	C. Wheeler	Mrs E. A. Widdis	3:28.25
1914	Kingsburgh	4 h	George Meddick	Isaac Foulsham	L. K. S. Mackinnon	3:26.00
1913	Posinatus	5 g	A. Shanahan	J. Chambers	J. Chambers	3:31.00
1912	Piastre	4 h	A. Shanahan	R. O'Connor	W. Brown	3:27.50
1911	The Parisian	6 g	R. Cameron	C. Wheeler	J. F. Kirby	3:27.75
1910	Comedy King	4 h	William McLachlan	James Lynch	Sol Green	3:27.75
1909	Prince Foote	3 c	William McLachlan	Frank McGrath	John Brown	3:27.50
1908	Lord Nolan	3 c	J. R. Flynn	E. A. Mayo	J. Mayo	3:28.75
1907	Apologue	5 h	Bill Evans	Isaac Earnshaw	R. L. Cleland	3:27.50
1906	Poseidon	3 c	Tom Clayton	Isaac Earnshaw	Sir Hugh Denison	3:31.25
1905	Blue Spec	6 h	Frank Bullock	Walter Hickenbotham	P. A. Connolly	3:27.50
1904	Acrasia	7 m	Tom Clayton	A. E. Wills	H. Oxenham	3:28.25
1903	Lord Cardigan	3 c	Norman Godby	A. E. Cornwell	J. Mayo	3:29.25
1902	The Victory	4 h	Bobby Lewis	Richard Bradfield	W. Clark & L. Robinson	3:29.00
1901	Revenue	5 g	Frederick J. Dunn	Hugh Munro	C. Leslie Macdonald	3:30.50
1900	Clean Sweep	3 c	Andrew Richardson	James Scobie	John Cumming	3:29.00
1899	Merriwee	3 c	V. Turner	James Wilson, Jr.	Herbert Power	3:36.50

YEAR	WINNER	AGE SEX	JOCKEY	TRAINER	OWNER	TIME
1898	The Grafter	5 g	John Gough	William 'Black Bill' Forrester	William 'Black Bill' Forrester	3:29.75
1897	Gaulus	6 h	Stephen Callinan	William 'Black Bill' Forrester	William 'Black Bill' Forrester	3:31.00
1896	Newhaven	3 c	H. J. Gardiner	Walter Hickenbotham	W. T. Jones & S. Cooper	3:28.50
1895	Auraria	3 f	J. Stevenson	J. H. Hill	D. James	3:29.00
1894	Patron	4 h	Henry G. Dawes	Richard Bradfield	F. W. Purches	3:31.00
1893	Tarcoola	7 h	Herbert Cripps	Joseph Cripps	J. D. Lewis	3:30.50
1892	Glenloth	5 h	G. Robson	M. Carmody	M. Carmody	3:36.25
1891	Malvolio	4 h	G. Redfearn	J. Redfearn	J. Redfearn	3:29.25
1890	Carbine	5 h	Robert Ramage	Walter Hickenbotham	D. S. Wallace	3:28.25
1889	Bravo	6 h	James Anwin	T. Wilson	W. T. Jones	3:32.50
1888	Mentor	4 h	Mick O'Brien	Walter Hickenbotham	D. S. Wallace	3:30.75
1887	Dunlop	5 h	Tommy Sanders	J. Nicholson	R. Donovan	3:28.50
1886	Arsenal	4 h	W. English	H. Rayner	W. Gannon	3:31.00
1885	Sheet Anchor	7 h	Mick O'Brien	T. Wilson	Martin Loughlin	3:29.50
1884	Malua	5 h	Alick Robertson	Isaac Foulsham	J. O. Inglis	3:31.75
1883	Martini-Henry	3 c	J. Williamson	Michael Fennelly	Hon. James White	3:30.50
1882	The Assyrian	5 h	C. Hutchins	J. E. Savill	J. E. Savill	3:40.00
1881	Zulu	4 h	Jim Gough	T. Lamond	C. McDonnell	3:32.50
1880	Grand Flaneur	3 c	Thomas Hales	T. Brown	William A. Long	3:34.75

Year	Horse	Wt	Jockey	Trainer	Owner	Time
1879	Darriwell	5 h	S. Cracknell	W. E. Dakin	W. A Guesdon [20]	3:30.75
1878	Calamia	5 h	T. Brown	Etienne de Mestre	Etienne de Mestre	3:35.75
1877	Chester	3 c	P. Pigott	Etienne de Mestre	Hon. James White	3:33.50
1876	Briseis	3 f	Peter St. Albans	James Wilson, Sr.	James Wilson, Sr.	3:36.25
1875	Wollomai	6 h	R. Batty	S. Moon	J. Cleeland	3:38.00
1874	Haricot	4 g	P. Pigott	S. Harding	A. Chirnside	3:37.50
1873	Don Juan	4 h	W. Wilson	James Wilson, Sr.	W. Johnstone	3:36.00
1872	The Quack	6 h	W. Enderson	John Tait	John Tait	3:39.00
1871	The Pearl	5 h	J. Cavanagh	John Tait	John Tait	3:39.00
1870	Nimblefoot	7 g	J. Day	W. Lang	W. Craig	3:37.00
1869	Warrior	6 g	J. Morrison	R. Sevior	A. Saqui	3:40.00
1868	Glencoe	4 h	C. Stanley	John Tait	John Tait	3:42.00
1867	Tim Whiffler	5 h	John Driscoll	Etienne de Mestre	Etienne de Mestre	3:39.00
1866	The Barb	3 c	W. Davis	John Tait	John Tait	3:43.00
1865	Toryboy	8 g	E. Cavanagh	P. Miley	B. Marshall	3:44.00
1864	Lantern	3 c	S. Davis	S. Mahon	H. Fisher	3:52.00
1863	Banker	3 c	H. Chifney	Sam Waldock	J. Harper	3:44.00
1862	Archer	6 h	John Cutts	Etienne de Mestre	Etienne de Mestre	3:47.00
1861	Archer	5 h	John Cutts	Etienne de Mestre	Etienne de Mestre	3:52.00

YEAR	WINNER	WEIGHT (KG)	SP	SECOND	THIRD	FIELD
2020						
2019						
2018						
2017						
2016						
2015	Prince Of Penzance	53.0	$101	Max Dynamite	Criterion	24
2014	Protectionist	56.5	$14	Red Cadeaux	Who Shot The Barman	22
2013	Fiorente	55	$7f	Red Cadeaux	Mount Athos	24
2012	Green Moon	53.5	$20	Fiorente	Jakkalberry	24
2011	Dunaden	54.5	$7	Red Cadeaux	Lucas Cranach	23
2010	Americain	54.5	$11	Maluckyday	So You Think	23
2009	Shocking	51	$10	Crime Scene	Mourilyan	23
2008	Viewed	53	$41	Bauer	C'est La Guerre	22
2007	Efficient	54.5	$17	Purple Moon	Mahler	21
2006	Delta Blues	56.9	$18	Pop Rock	Maybe Better	23
2005	Makybe Diva	58	$4.4f	On A Jeune	Xcellent	24
2004	Makybe Diva	55.5	$3.6f	Vinnie Roe	Zazzman	24
2003	Makybe Diva	51	$8	She's Archie	Jardine'sLookout	23
2002	Media Puzzle	52.5	$6.50	Mr. Prudent	Beekeeper	23
2001	Ethereal	52	$10	Give The Slip	Persian Punch	22

1999	Rogan Josh	50	5/1	Central Park	Zazabelle/ Lahar *	24
1998	Jezabeel	51	6/1f	Champagne	Persian Punch	24
1997	Might and Power	56	7/2f	Doriemus	Markham	22
1996	Saintly	55.5	8/1	Count Chivas	Skybeau	22
1995	Doriemus	54.5	10/1	Nothin' Leica Dane	Vintage Crop	21
1994	Jeune	56.5	16/1	Paris Lane	Oompala	24
1993	Vintage Crop	55.5	4/1	TeAkauNick	Mercator	24
1992	Subzero	54.5	14/1	Veandercross	Castletown	21
1991	Let's Elope	51	3/1f	Shiva's Revenge	Magnolia Hall	24
1990	Kingston Rule	53	7/1f	The Phantom	Mr. Brooker	24
1989	Tawrrific	54	30/1	Super Impose	Kudz	23
1988	Empire Rose	53.5	5/1f	Natski	Na Botto	22
1987	Kensei	51.5	12/1	Empire Rose	Rosedale	21
1986	At Talaq	54.5	10/1	Rising Fear	Sea Legend	22
1985	What A Nuisance	52.5	15/1	Koiro Corrie May	Tripsacum	23
1984	Black Knight	50	10/1	Chagemar	Mapperley Heights	19
1983	Kiwi	52	9/1	Noble Comment	Mr. Jazz	24
1982	Gurner's Lane	56	8/1	Kingston Town	Noble Comment	23
1981	Just A Dash	53.5	15/1	El Laurena	Flashing Light	22

*dead heat for third

Year	Winner	Weight	Odds	Second	Third	Starters
1980	Beldale Ball	49.5	11/1	My Blue Denim	Love Bandit	22
1979	Hyperno	56	7/1	Salamander	Red Nose	22
1978	Arwon	50.5	5/1	Dandaleith	Karu	22
1977	Gold and Black	57	7/2f	Reckless	Hyperno	24
1976	Van der Hum	54.5	9/2f	Gold And Black	Kythera	23
1975	Think Big	58.5	33/1	Holiday Waggon	Medici	20
1974	Think Big	53	12/1	Leilani	Captain Peri	22
1973	Gala Supreme	49	9/1	Glengowan	Daneson	24
1972	Piping Lane	48	40/1	Magnifique	Gunsynd	22
1971	Silver Knight	8.9	10/1	Igloo	Tails	21
1970	Baghdad Note	8.7	25/1	Vansittart	Clear Prince	23
1969	Rain Lover	9.7	8/1	Alsop	Ben Lomond	23
1968	Rain Lover	8.2	7/1	Fileur	Fans	26
1967	Red Handed	8.9	4/1ef	Red Crest	Floodbird	22
1966	Galilee	8.13	11/2f	Light Fingers	Duo	22
1965	Light Fingers	8.4	15/1	Ziema	Midlander	26
1964	Polo Prince	8.3	12/1	Elkayel	Welltown	26
1963	Gatum	7.12	25/1	Ilumquh	Grand Print	26
1962	Even Stevens	8.5	3/1f	Comicquita	Aquanita	26
1961	Lord Fury	7.8	20/1	Grand Print	Dhaulagiri	25
1960	Hi Jinx	7.1	50/1	Howsie	Ilumquh	32

Year	Winner	Wt	Odds	2nd	3rd	Starters
1958	Baystone	8.9	10/1	Monte Carlo	Red Pine	29
1957	Straight Draw	8.5	13/2	Prince Darius	Pandie Sun	19
1956	Evening Peal	8.0	15/1	Redcraze	Caranna	22
1955	Toparoa	7.8	6/1	Rising Fast	Sir William	24
1954	Rising Fast	9.5	5/2f	Hellion	Gay Helios	25
1953	Wodalla	8.4	14/1	Most Regal	My Hero	21
1952	Dalray	9.8	5/1f	Welkin Sun	Reformed	30
1951	Delta	9.5	10/1	Akbar	Double Blank	28
1950	Comic Court	9.5	25/1	Chiquita	Morse Code	26
1949	Foxzami	8.8	16/1	Hoyle	Benvolo	31
1948	Rimfire	7.2	80/1	Dark Marne	Saxony	30
1947	Hiraji	7.11	12/1	Fresh Boy	Red Fury	30
1946	Russia	9.0	16/1	On Target	Carey	35
1945	Rainbird	7.7	12/1	Silver Link	Leonard	26
1944	Sirius	8.5	3/1f	Peter	Cellini	23
1943	Dark Felt	8.4	7/2ef	Counsel	Claudette	24
1942	Colonus	7.2	33/1	Phocion	Heart's Desire	24
1941	Skipton	7.7	8/1	Son Of Aurous	Beau Vite	23
1940	Old Rowley	7.12	100/1	Maikai	Tidal Wave	20
1939	Rivette	7.9	5/1f	Maikai	Pantler	26
1938	Catalogue	8.4	25/1	Bourbon	Ortelle's Star	22

1937	The Trump	8.5	11/2ef	Willie Win	Sarcherie	28
1936	Wotan	7.11	100/1	Silver Standard	Balkan Prince	20
1935	Marabou	7.11	9/2f	Sarcherie	Sylvandale	22
1934	Peter Pan	9.1	14/1	Sarcherie	Latrobe	22
1933	Hall Mark	7.8	4/1	Shadow King	Gaine Carrington/Topical *	18
1932	Peter Pan	7.6	4/1f	Yarramba	Shadow King	27
1931	White Nose	6.12	8/1	Shadow King	Concentrate	14
1930	Phar Lap	9.12	8/11f	Second Wind	Shadow King	15
1929	Nightmarch	9.2	6/1	Paquito	Phar Lap	14
1928	Statesman	8.0	7/2	Strephon	Demost	17
1927	Trivalve	7.6	6/1	Silvius	Son 'o Mine	26
1926	Spearfelt	9.3	10/1	Naos	Pan Theon	21
1925	Windbag	9.2	5/1	Manfred	Pilliwinkie	28
1924	Backwood	8.2	8/1	Stand By	Spearfelt	18
1923	Bitalli	7.0	4/1f	Rivoli	Accarak	26
1922	King Ingoda	7.1	8/1	The Cypher	Mufti	32
1921	Sister Olive	6.9	16/1	The Rover	Amazonia	25
1920	Poitrel	10	8/1	Erasmus	Queen Comedy	23
1919	Artilleryman	7.6	10/1	Richmond Main	Two Blues	20

*dead heat for third

1917	Westcourt	8.5	4/1	Lingle	Wallace Isingla	20
1916	Sasanof	6.12	12/1	Shepherd King	St Spasa	28
1915	Patrobas	7.6	8/1	Westcourt	Carlita	24
1914	Kingsburgh	6.12	20/1	Sir Alwynton	Moonbria	28
1913	Posinatus	7.1	15/1	Belove	Ulva's Isle	20
1912	Piastre	7.9	7/1	Hallowmas	Uncle Sam	23
1911	The Parisian	8.9	5/1	Flavian	Didus	33
1910	Comedy King	7.11	10/1	Trafalgar	Apple Pie	30
1909	Prince Foote	7.8	4/1ef	Alawa	Aberdeen	26
1908	Lord Nolan	6.1	16/1	Tulkeroo	Delaware	22
1907	Apologue	7.9	3/1f	Mooltan	Mountain King	19
1906	Poseidon	7.6	4/1	Antonious	Proceed	21
1905	Blue Spec	8.0	10/1	Scot Free	Tartan	27
1904	Acrasia	7.6	14/1	Lord Cardigan	Blinker	34
1903	Lord Cardigan	6.8	5/1	Wakeful	Seaport	24
1902	The Victory	8.12	25/1	Vanity Fair	Abundance	22
1901	Revenue	7.1	7/4f	San Fran	Khaki	19
1900	Clean Sweep	7.0	20/1	Maltster	Alix	29
1899	Merriwee	7.6	7/1ef	Voyou	Dewey	28
1898	The Grafter	9.2	8/1	Wait-a-bit	Cocos	28
1897	Gaulus	7.8	14/1	The Grafter	Aurum	29

1896	Newhaven	7.13	4/1f	Bloodshot	The Skipper	25
1895	Auraria	7.4	33/1	Hova	Burrabari	36
1894	Patron	9.3	33/1	Devon	Nada	28
1893	Tarcoola	8.4	40/1	Carnage	Jeweller	30
1892	Glenloth	7.13	50/1	Ronda	Penance	35
1891	Malvolio	8.4	16/1	Sir William	Strathmore	34
1890	Carbine	10.5	4/1f	Highborn	Correze	39
1889	Bravo	8.7	8/1	Carbine	Melos	20
1888	Mentor	8.3	7/1	Tradition	The Yeoman	28
1887	Dunlop	8.3	20/1	Silvermine	Australian Peer	18
1886	Arsenal	7.5	20/1	Trenton	Silvermine	28
1885	Sheet Anchor	7.11	20/1	Grace Darling	Trenton	35
1884	Malua	9.9	6/1	Commotion	Plausible	24
1883	Martini-Henry	7.5	5/1f	First Water	Commotion	29
1882	The Assyrian	7.13	33/1	Stockwell	Gudarz	25
1881	Zulu	5.1	50/1	The Czar	Sweetmeat	33
1880	Grand Flaneur	6.1	4/1	Progress	Lord Burghley	22
1879	Darriwell	7.4	33/1	Sweetmeat	Suwarrow	27
1878	Calamia	8.2	10/1	Tom Kirk	Waxy	30
1877	Chester	6.12	5/1	Savanaka	The Vagabond	33
1876	Briseis	6.4	13/2	Sibyl	Timothy	33

1874	Haricot	6.7	16/1	Protos	The Diver	18
1873	Don Juan	6.12	3/1f	Dagworth	Horatio	24
1872	The Quack	7.1	11/2	The Ace	Dagworth	22
1871	The Pearl	7.3	100/1	Romula	Irish King	23
1870	Nimblefoot	6.3	12/1	Lapdog	Valentine	28
1869	Warrior	8.1	10/1	The Monk	Phoebe	26
1868	Glencoe	9.1	10/1	Strop	Shenandoah	25
1867	Tim Whiffler	8.11	5/2f	Queen Of Hearts	Exile	27
1866	The Barb	6.11	6/1f	Exile	Falcon	28
1865	Toryboy	7.0	25/1	Panic	Riverina	23
1864	Lantern	6.3	15/1	Poet	Rose Of Denmark	19
1863	Banker	5.4	10/1	Musidora	Rose Of Denmark	7
1862	Archer	10.2	2/1f	Mormon	Camden	20
1861	Archer	9.7	6/1	Mormon	Prince	17

Dedication
FOR DAD

About the Author

Paddy O'Reilly is a former amateur jockey, hobby trainer and SP bookmaker. He once dreamed of riding a Melbourne Cup winner, and then of training one but, like the rest of the country, now settles for backing the winner on the first Tuesday in November. This book is the culmination of a lifelong fascination with the race, and the collection of many of the records, stories and trivia featured within these pages.

First published in 2016 by New Holland Publishers Pty Ltd
London • Sydney • Auckland

The Chandlery Unit 704 50 Westminster Bridge Road London SE1 7QY
United Kingdom
1/66 Gibbes Street Chatswood NSW 2067 Australia
5/39 Woodside Ave Northcote, Auckland 0627 New Zealand

www.newhollandpublishers.com

A record of this book is held at the British Library and the National Library
of Australia.

ISBN 9781742579054

Managing Director: Fiona Schultz
Publisher: Alan Whiticker
Design: Andrew Davies
Cover Design: Andrew Quinlan
Production Director: James Mills-Hicks
Printer: Ligare Book Printers, Melbourne, Victoria

10 9 8 7 6 5 4 3 2 1

Keep up with New Holland Publishers on Facebook
www.facebook.com/NewHollandPublishers